PRAISE for *FIVE WOMEN IN A JEEP*

Intimate and illuminating, this collection of essays invites readers into a deeper engagement with their own daily moments. Priscilla masterfully weaves timeless Buddhist teachings into the fabric of ordinary experience, revealing how ancient wisdom can guide us through life's challenges and illuminate our shared humanity. Her years of practice and contemplation shine through each page, offering profound insights that feel both accessible and transformative. Beautiful and wise—this book deserves a leisurely read, allowing each essay to settle and reveal what may be true for you as well.

—Patti Holland, MS, CRC, NBC-HWC

Asst. Professor of the Practice and Asst. Director of Mindfulness Education, School of Professional Studies and the Mindfulness Center at Brown University

This charming little dharma book is filled with wit and heartfelt wisdom, woven through personal stories. A wonderful read for anyone on the meditation or dharma path! —Janka Livoncova

Guiding Teacher, Chattanooga Insight Meditation Community; Core Teacher, Sacred Mountain Sangha; Somatic Movement Educator

Five Women in a Jeep

and Other Musings of a Meditator

Priscilla Szneke

Visit our website at **www.StillwaterPress.com** for more information.

First Stillwater River Publications Edition

ISBN: 978-1-968548-04-9

Library of Congress Control Number: 2025918174

1 2 3 4 5 6 7 8 9 10

Publisher's Cataloging-in-Publication
Provided by Cassidy Cataloguing Services, Inc.

Names: Szneke, Priscilla, author.
Title: Five women in a jeep : and other musings of a meditator /
Priscilla Szneke.
Description: First Stillwater River Publications edition. | West
Warwick, RI, USA : Stillwater River Publications, [2025]
Identifiers: LCCN: 2025918174 | ISBN: 9781968548049
Subjects: LCSH: Buddhism. | Self-consciousness (Awareness)
| Mindfulness (Psychology) | Spiritual healing. | LCGFT:
Essays. | Self-help publications.
Classification: LCC: BQ4055 .S96 2025 | DDC: 294.3--dc23

Written by Priscilla Szneke.
Front cover illustration by Elizabeth Bessette.
Cover and interior design by Elisha Gillette.

DISCLAIMER

The author of this book does not offer or provide medical advice or prescribe the use of anything in this book as a form of treatment for medical, mental, or physical problems.

TABLE OF CONTENTS

AUTHOR'S NOTE

NO SINGLE STORY OR NARRATIVE CAN FULLY CAP-
ture the complexity of a human life. Each story we tell
is made up of moments, coming together, constantly
changing, arising, and falling away. Sometimes those
moments look familiar. Others are outside our own
lived reality. The stories in this book are written from a
particular perspective: that of an older, privileged, white
female, and they are essentially true, although some
details may have been modified or excluded to create
a clearer picture or idea. Many, but not all, names have
been changed. But most importantly, all these events
are in the past, and these stories are not in sequential
order. Each reflects one moment in time. And just as I
am different from who I was a month ago, so are you.

You might also notice that strategies and insights are
repeated in some of these essays because my conditioned
responses and habitual patterns show up in different
ways. They can be very sneaky, but bringing awareness
to them is how I began to work with them.

Also included are descriptions of a few different types of meditations. All meditations are good and are part of many spiritual traditions. I simply emphasized some of the most common ones in the insight (Vipassana) tradition, which is the type of meditation I practice.

ACKNOWLEDGMENTS

THIS PAGE SHOULD BE ENTITLED AUTHORS AND not Acknowledgments because I did not write this book. It was a seed of an idea, and once planted, it had a life of its own. A life that included the participation of many people. But it's like that with everything in life, whether a book, a company, or an athletic endeavor. We don't ever do it alone. Our goals and dreams are supported, buoyed, challenged, taught, and directed by many, some who came before us and others in our immediate circle and others far from that circle, all making a difference in our lives.

Here is an incomplete list of people who made that difference in my life and directly impacted the creation of this book.

Much appreciation to Pascal Auclair, Elizabeth Bessette, Rebecca Bradshaw, Anna Douglas, John Estes, Gil Fronsdal, Patricia Holland, Janka Livoncova, Roger Lopata, Louis Mariorenzi, Jane Metzger, Stephanie Szneke, and the Willet Library Tuesday Writing Group.

And to those not listed here, I am ever so grateful to you. You will reside in my heart always.

DEDICATION

To all sentient beings.
May we all feel safe, be happy, and live with ease.

Pay attention. Be astonished. Tell about it.
—Mary Oliver

1

SHIFTING PERSPECTIVE

Don't see something as a problem. Just see it as it is.
—Sayadawa U Tejaniya

MY FIRST YOGA CLASS

THE THIRTY-BY-TWENTY-FOOT ROOM IS PACKED with people dressed in spandex and tights in a variety of colors. Mostly women, they range in age from twenty to fifty. The heat in the room is set to ninety-five degrees. "Get a mat and put it near the wall so that you can follow my instructions during the yoga class," said Philip, the teacher leading the class.

I'm not thrilled to be here, but I am not particularly intimidated either, even though I am one of the older students. I'm in good physical shape - I play tennis, sail, bike, and hike. I do all these things not so much to be fit but to calm my mind. I have a short attention span and am hyperactive. Not only am I unfocused and restless if I don't exercise, but I also become angry, impatient, and confused. There must be some diagnosis for that.

I'm taking this yoga class because I have a back injury, and my physical therapist forbids me from doing anything active. I'm supposed to allow my back to rest and heal, and the type of dynamic movement I am used to is not conducive to healing. Truth be told, my PT didn't want me to do much of anything, but I fought with her until she relented. She allowed me to take a yoga class, but it was to be one that was gentle, perhaps a beginner class. I didn't tell her I found the most vigorous yoga class in my area and strolled in.

So far, so good. Now it's time to start the class, and the teacher leads us into the first pose. U2's "Beautiful Day" plays in the background.

"It's a beautiful day. Don't let it get away."

Philip asks us to kneel on our mats, then bring our butts to our heels, chest forward to meet our thighs, foreheads on the floor, and arms alongside our bodies. He calls this child's pose.

I move into the pose. As I pause here, I can feel my body connected not only to the earth but also to itself. I am still, but I can feel my breath rocking my body and notice the beat of my heart.

I burst into tears. What the hell? Why am I crying? My life, at least from the outside, was storybook perfect. I have a good marriage, a beautiful home, a privileged life, and a job that I enjoy that gives me enough time to pursue other interests. I try to calm myself down so no one will notice that I am a bundle of tears, but it doesn't really matter because the room is so hot and we're already so sweaty that no one notices I am crying. But why am I crying?

"The heart is a bloom. Shoots up through the stony ground."

I chose this class because I wanted vigorous movement, and that's what I'm getting. I need to call on all the strength and attention I can muster to move from one pose to the next. Occasionally, we are told to hold certain poses for extended periods of time. Keeping my arms lifted and parallel to the floor with my right knee bent for three minutes takes focus, flexibility, and endurance. I can feel every contracted muscle in my body. And although it was difficult, I'm able to do most of the class and feel proud of myself.

At the end of class, we take child's pose again. As I move into this position of limbs against torso against limbs, I feel so connected with my body. I pause and become still. I notice the rhythm of my breath and heartbeat again, the quiet music being played, the smell of sweat, and the release of tension. Once again, I start crying. What is happening? I feel relieved, having spent all the stress and restlessness I came in with. And yet, I am crying.

Being with myself in stillness was something I usually avoided. And here I found it calming and healing. What is happening in this somatic experience of pause and restfulness? This place of quiet and calm. I'm determined to find out.

"Touch me. Take me to that other place."

COMPASSION

"IT'S DIFFICULT TO SEE BECKY STRUGGLING," JANE said.

Jane and I were enjoying one of our monthly lunch dates, and the talk had turned to a friend who was having difficulty with her husband's relapse into addiction. Jane expressed her sorrow. I thought that the situation didn't need to be as difficult as Becky was making it.

"Maybe Becky should talk to a therapist," I suggested. "Or she should step back and see the situation from a different perspective. Maybe she should just confront her husband or give him an ultimatum."

I continued offering other ideas, trying to figure out how I could fix our friend's dilemma. When I paused for a breath and looked at Jane's face, she looked puzzled. In that moment, I realized that she had come to the conversation with compassion for Becky, and I had come with judgment and a bunch of possible solutions to fix a problem that was not mine.

Jane is my teacher when it comes to compassion.

Once when we were out, she paused to chat with the homeless person occupying a stoop in Wayland Square, giving him a few dollars. "I always say hello to him when I see him," she said as we walked away.

Compassion, or care toward oneself and others when we or they are suffering, is one of the most important tenets in mindfulness and in life. Cultivating kindness and care when things are difficult, first towards oneself and then eventually towards others, is a game-changer because life can be very, very difficult, and unless we nurture this tender-heartedness, we can get caught up in recrimination, self-doubt, blame, or shame.

This was evident when I was teaching compassion along with the other heart practices (kindness, compassion, joy, and equanimity) in a yoga teacher training program. One of the participants, who does chaplaincy work at a local Catholic college, was flabbergasted when we did a meditation with the intention of sending compassion to ourselves. She said that it was part of her job to actively practice compassion towards others, but the thought never occurred to her to practice it for herself.

When I was first introduced to the Heart Practices at a retreat, it was compassion that challenged me the most. It was simply too uncomfortable to be with difficulty and suffering, mine or others. I wanted a way out of the discomfort, and one way out was to try to fix it. Just like I wanted to fix Becky's situation.

At first, it felt awkward to do a compassion practice.

Often, we use phrases to ground us in the practice, and this also allows us to see what thoughts, feelings, and sensations arise. I started by repeating the phrases. *"May I be free from suffering and the causes of suffering,"* and simply noticed what arose: sadness, fear, restlessness, tightness in the belly and throat. And in doing so, I started to become aware of the discomfort, without pushing it away. I also noticed its changing nature. Sadness changed to sorrow, fear to curiosity, restlessness to ease, back to restlessness, and tightness to movement in the belly and throat. In this way, I am present for myself, establishing the foundation to eventually be present for others in an open-hearted way.

"It's difficult to see Becky struggling," Jane said again.

"Yes, it is," I replied. "Let's call her and see how she is."

THOUGHT FULL OR
THOUGHTFUL MIND

"I can't meditate."

That was my first reaction after attempting my first formal sitting meditation practice. I was so caught up with all the thoughts in my mind that wanted my attention. It was like trying to gather 1000 children who were all yelling and jumping around all at the same time to sit down and be quiet. Not happening.

I've spoken with numerous people since then who have had this same experience, convinced that they can't meditate. This is due to a widely held misconception that during meditation, we need to empty our minds of thoughts. But that's not what mindfulness meditation asks us to do. Instead, it asks us to pay attention to those thoughts in a particular way. When we pause to pay attention with curiosity and some objectivity, we see that not only are there thousands of thoughts, but they are incessant. What a great discovery! The mind is designed to think, and by becoming aware of your thoughts, you can understand how you think and how those thoughts influence you.

Thoughts arise in the mind due to causes and conditions. The process of thinking has a function just like the other organs in the body. The kidneys filter fluids to excrete excessive or toxic materials, and the heart increases its rate when exercising so that muscles can get more oxygen. It's the same with the mind. It gets information and stores it, then compares it to experiences it has saved in its databank to determine how to respond to it. It does this on its own, functioning just like the heart and the kidneys do. We can allow the mind to think without getting caught up in the thought-filled mind. We can simply observe the thoughts as they arise and pass away.

I now begin my meditation practice by asking, *"Where is my attention right now?"* Once I establish where my attention is, I can decide where I want to direct it. I might notice that my attention is on thinking, thinking, thinking, and again trying to settle and organize those 1000 children. What better supports me is directing my attention to the sensations of breathing. Not to the mind thinking about breathing, but to the actual sensations of breathing. Maybe feeling the breath in the belly or chest, base of the nose, or back of the throat. Expansion, contraction, pause, deep, shallow, in, out, and any other sensations that might be present so that when you breathe, you know you are breathing.

And then not too long into the practice, I get distracted again. When I notice that I am distracted, I know where my attention is, and that is mindfulness. I note or label the thinking as thinking, aware of it but not carried away by it. Then I can gently redirect the attention back to the sensations of breathing.

When I practice in this way, I cultivate one-pointed or focused, non-judgmental attention by bringing my awareness back to the sensations of breathing again and again. I make this choice of where I want my attention to be and allow other aspects of my experience to be in the background. I don't get rid of anything.

As I observe what is happening in my experience as I meditate, I notice I can still get distracted. My mind doesn't like to be observed and dismissed! Sometimes the thoughts get louder and more insistent, just like an obstinate child that wants its mother's attention. And so, I bring care to it each time I'm distracted, but also create a boundary. "Yes, I hear you. No, not now."

So, if you are meditating and your mind is full of thoughts, don't try to get rid of them. Simply be aware of what is happening in your experience in a kind way and use the sensations of breathing as an anchor rather than getting caught up in the thinking mind or its commentary. In this way, you are being thoughtful about your thought-filled mind.

EMBODIED

*This is my head. It thinks. It talks. It charms. It wor-
ries. It laughs. It hurts. It has a hundred wonderful
tricks. I am proud of it.*

*This is my body. It is funny-looking. It malfunc-
tions. It looks best in winter clothes. I have as little
to do with it as is humanly possible. Lucky for my
body that I need it to chauffeur my head around.
Otherwise, out it would go.*

THIS BIT OF SATIRE WAS WRITTEN BY ALAN RICK-
man, and I think it epitomizes how we are not in relationship to our bodies. As this suggests, we tend to live
in our heads. We've learned early on to identify with our
thoughts and emotions, giving credence to worry and
regret or the distractions of fantasy and desires. We value
our minds over any other aspect of our beings, even if
it causes us suffering and distress. And by doing so, we
exist on the margins of our lives. James Joyce described

this relationship well when he wrote, *"Mr. Duffy lived a short distance from his body."*

We are embodied beings. Our sense of touch, smell, taste, sight, and hearing are how we take in information, enjoy, and interact with the world in the present moment. It is how we know and navigate the world, how we come to experience it as it happens, rather than through our memories or how we want it to be.

In teaching mindfulness-based interventions over the past fifteen years, I have noticed how, over this period of time, people have disconnected more and more from their bodies. The very first practice in the Mindfulness-based Stress Reduction program is a body scan, where we notice the different sensations that arise and change in the body, and few people have the vocabulary to express those sensations. I offer some suggestions. Warmth, coolness, pressure, constriction, expansion, pulsation, movement, spaciousness, sensitivity, achy, tenseness, fluttery, wobbly are only a few possibilities. And no sensation is possible as well. But the inability to experience any of these, except the last one, suggests we have lost an immediate and important part of our lives.

Our society has become dependent on that quick adrenaline rush created by the ubiquitous multiple distractions that surround us. And when we aren't getting that rush, we complain that we are bored. But is it boredom that we are experiencing? It may simply be peace or calm, states that seem elusive to many of us because we don't recognize them anymore when they arise. Perhaps the gratification and depth of knowledge we can obtain by being with what some might call the boring may result in profound joy, insight, or awe. What if we stay with and investigate this state of boredom and how it manifests in our body with curiosity, get to know it better, even become intimate with it?

A few years into my practice, I became intimate with my anxiety in this way. I was plagued by anxiety. It took different forms: distress, worry, restlessness, and catastrophic thinking. And it was difficult to be with as I tried to ignore, push away, or distract myself from it. What was the somatic manifestation of this anxiety? One manifestation was constriction in my chest just below the breastbone. If I took long, deep breaths, it dissipated. Another time, I noticed that anxiety manifested in my upper chest and throat. More constriction. My breath was short and shallow, and my throat felt tight. When I took deep breaths, it didn't go away, but I was able to stay with it and noticed it changing. Sometimes strengthen, sometimes lessen. Watching it change allowed me to get curious about it even though I couldn't make it go away. I just stayed with it until it decided to dissipate on its own, which it eventually did. I learned that my anxiety came and went. It wasn't always there.

Dogen-Zengi, a Zen master from Japan who lived in the 13th century, is quoted as saying, *"To be enlightened is to be intimate with all things."* He is suggesting that enlightenment is about connecting with what is present, rather than some lofty, spiritual goal. And the only way to do that is through our senses and our body, which are immediate and direct.

SPACIOUS AWARENESS

"There's a boat coming up on your port side," my teammate said as I helmed this small, eighteen-foot sailboat around the racecourse.

"Yes, I know, I can hear it," I replied.

When we got back to the dock, my teammate said, *"You have really good spatial awareness. I was surprised that you were aware of the boat coming up behind you."*

"Thanks!" I replied.

But it's not good spatial awareness that I have. What I have is good, *spacious* awareness. And meditation taught me that.

I have a confession to make. I am a terrible meditator. That was especially evident when I first started meditating. At that time, I was taught to do a concentration practice by narrowly focusing my attention on the sensations of breathing. My meditation teacher suggested that every time I got distracted, I recognize it and return my attention to the breath. I was getting dizzy from pinging from the breath to a thought, back to the breath, back to a thought again and again, all happening in one nano-second. And that doesn't include the restlessness and aversion that were erupting as I was pinging.

Even after completing a one-month retreat and finally being able to be still for a while, I had to negotiate with my mind to stay seated for my daily thirty-minute meditation. Somewhere from the deep recesses of my mind, a voice would announce loudly and clearly after about twenty minutes that I was *done*. So, my mind and I agreed that we would simply sit together for another ten minutes. I had my eyes open, but I stealthily focused my attention on a paint chip on the wall for the duration.

I've gotten better with more practice. Many hours on the cushion and on retreat have taught my body that it has the capacity to be still for long periods of time and that focusing one's attention can be learned… sort of. This concentration practice, or a focused attention practice on the sensations of breathing, is foundational, but you can use other objects as a focus of attention, and what works best for me is expanding my field of attention by using either sound or the sensations of the whole body sitting. With that slight opening of awareness, I feel less constricted and tight.

The intention of a concentration practice in the tradition I practice in, is to settle the mind so that wisdom can arise. But for wisdom to arise, we need to see clearly. We need to be present for our full experience in a particular way, without judgment, not just for our breath.

Widening the lens of awareness even further, perhaps anchored to the breath but not focusing on it exclusively, we can pay attention to what is happening around us without getting caught up or pushing away one aspect of our experience over the other. We can be present for the thought, emotion, sight, sound, or anything else that arises in this spacious awareness. What we're training our mind to do is maintain presence with what actually is, without jumping onto the train of associations or reactivity, riding the waves of our thoughts, and not losing our connection with the present moment.

When I was helming the boat, I was aware of the wind on my face, telling me what direction it was coming from and how strong it was. I could hear the boat behind me because of the subtle sounds of waves slapping against its hull growing louder as it approached us. I could feel the boat I was in responding as I moved the helm. I could see where the finish line was, and I was able to stay ahead of the boat behind me. I could smell the ocean as I felt the joy of being in nature. Noticing in this way, fully present without preference or judgment, enabled me to not only be aware of my surroundings and my position relative to them, such as location, distance, and personal space (spatial awareness), but to also cultivate an open focus that included whatever was arising in my experience moment to moment (spacious awareness). Sensations, feelings, emotions, thoughts, sounds, breath. All arising and passing away like clouds in the sky. Not preferring one over the other.

In seated meditation, it's the same thing. I don't need to choose any one sensory input or experience, but can be aware of the sounds of the birds outside, the itch on my shoulder, the expansiveness of the inbreath, and the pressure on my butt as I sit on my cushion. I recognize the emotion that arises with that itch (annoyance) and the thought that accompanies it (please go away) without getting caught up by it. I can notice if what I am experiencing is pleasant, unpleasant, or neutral without judgment. In this way, I am spaciously aware.

WISE VIEW

On retreat, we tend to prioritize sitting meditation, then walking meditation, and then activities of daily living. But on this one-month retreat, we followed a different philosophy and made daily activities paramount. Turning the usual paradigm around, we put our emphasis on being mindful of activities like showering, going to the bathroom, brushing teeth, walking, and doing our yogi job. We focused on mindfulness of activities of daily living because once we leave the retreat, we only do sitting meditation for short periods of time compared to the time we are interacting in the world. So, we practiced making sitting meditation the least important component of our day. With this small change in perspective came a seismic shift in my practice, even after I returned home from the retreat. Although mindfulness includes a non-judgmental attitude, I realized that I was subtly judging my sitting meditation practice and expecting it to be "better" than it was. But with this shift, I realized that I already bring mindfulness to my activities of daily life and therefore, was able to let go of this subtle, but pervasive, negative view about my sitting practice. This understanding enabled me to adopt a more balanced approach, reducing the unnecessary effort I typically exerted.

By shifting my perspective, I also let go of other judgments and biases I had, and the resulting spaciousness and relief in my life were palpable. The politician whom I railed against became a sad sack who simply didn't know better. That didn't excuse his actions, and it didn't mean I liked him, but there was more understanding and compassion for how he didn't know any other way of being, and he was only trying to find some happiness, just like me. I stopped railing against him.

I was able to let go of my dislike of many large businesses and corporations where employees are just a number, productivity is key, and certain protocols are instituted for efficiency, but strip away human interactions. I realized that it simply was the way it was, and could I find smaller vendors or companies to suit my needs? And if not, could I work within the system to get what I needed and maintain some objectivity?

And then looking in the mirror and accepting the aging process, rather than being unhappy seeing the effects of overexposure to the sun. For many summers, I played tennis at midday, and the effect of all those years exposed to the sun resulted in numerous wrinkles. Rather than regret, could I enjoy the memories of the times I had the privilege of playing on a historical grass court and the wonderful games that I won and lost?

I can spend time and energy avoiding, disliking, or wanting things to be different from what they are. Or I can shift my mindset to consider the situation differently, perhaps, by bringing in curiosity or stepping back to view things from a distance. It's like looking at an impressionistic painting. If I look at it from afar, it's a beautiful garden scene, but when I get close, it is simply strokes of a brush where no image exists. They are profoundly different and affect how we experience the painting itself. Knowing that there is always more than one viewpoint to our experience and that observing it from different angles is wisdom at work.

FINDING A PAUSE

I often begin my meditation practice by bringing my attention to the sensations of breathing. As I follow each inhale and exhale, I feel my body expand and contract. And there, at the end of my exhale, I often find a short pause. It is a moment of respite where I'm not getting caught up in runaway thoughts or emotions. Just a bit of space, a reprieve. Almost like taking a nap, refreshing. I would describe it as allowing whatever is happening in the moment to be just as it is. No pushing away or grasping anything. No thinking about it.

If I can find a moment of respite in my formal meditation practice, could I consciously find that pause in my day-to-day life?

A supervisor was ghosting me because she doesn't like conflict, and we had had a disagreement about scheduling. I needed at least partial resolution so that I could make decisions around other opportunities I had to teach. I was aggravated, uncomfortable, and looking for a way to express my annoyance. When I noticed my breathing was shallow, I intentionally elongated both the inhale and the exhale, and at the end of the exhale, I found that pause! And so, I took a few deep breaths to find a bit of calm. Supported by the long inhales and exhales, I rested in this pause. It was so much better than getting caught up in the aggrieved, frustrated vortex of wanting things to be different from what they were. It created a different quality to my experience; the pause created a calmness that is always welcome when it arises, even if it's only for a few seconds.

This idea of finding a pause came up again during a yoga class that I took. The teacher moved us through a sequence of challenging postures and repeated the sequence three times. Holding each one of the postures required a good amount of effort. And then, I heard my mind ask, "Where can I find a pause to rest?" In this situation, I found I could rest in the spaces between the poses, in the actual movement, where I found a release from the muscle contractions of the pose. Once again, I found that calm, albeit brief.

Once I found some space and calm around my situation with my supervisor, I was able to step back and evaluate. The understanding that this is how she interacts with others and that wasn't going to change allowed me to respond to her with clarity. I offered her an option and an end date to respond. If she didn't, I informed her I would be taking on other projects. I didn't hear from her, and so, I took on other projects.

This finding a pause in unpleasant or difficult situations also served me well in my yoga practice. Breathing and noticing the sensations in my body as I moved and held it all in awareness supported me through the postures and allowed me to notice and move towards any ease that might be present.

We tend to either push discomfort away or react to it. If I allow the discomfort to be in my awareness by acknowledging it, I can allow it to be there without pushing it away, and this allows me to find some spaciousness to hold the discomfort . Asking "where in this discomfort can I find a pause?" and seeing what arises.

SOLACE OF NATURE

I WAS INVOLVED IN A HUGE BUREAUCRATIC ENTAN-
glement that unfolded late on a Friday night and couldn't
be addressed until after the weekend. It was a mess, and I
was in New Hampshire on this Saturday morning at the
tail end of my vacation.

I was sitting at the kitchen table at the condominium,
distraught, but I knew that if I directed my attention to
the sensations of breathing, it would allow my mind to
come back to the present moment rather than spinning
off into the future, caught up in the worst-case scenario.
After a few moments of focusing on my breath, my nervous system settled down. As I brought my attention to
what was here and now, what I first noticed were all the
sounds outside the open window. I could hear a bird
singing vigorously in the distance. A red-eyed vireo
repeating de-wheat, de-wheat, deet-deet-deet, de-wheat,
deet-deet-deet. I also heard the occasional chip-chip trill
of the chipping sparrow. Then I noticed a strong but
pleasant woodsy fragrance. It was the smell of mulch,

newly placed in the beds around the condo. The heavy rains from the prior evening released the sweet smell into the air. I raised my head and looked out the window. There were a variety of different types of evergreens surrounding the building, mostly balsam fir, and a variety of deciduous trees, mature red maples, red spruce, and yellow birch, vigorous and tall.

Nature has always been a place of solace for me. It's soothed me on numerous occasions. Attending camp was a haven for me as a child and pre-adolescent, where I swam, learned archery, rode horses, and explored the woods. As an unhappy adolescent, I felt less reactive when I accompanied my parents to our local state parks on Sunday afternoons. And my daily sixty-minute hikes at retreat were integral in helping me settle into the routine of each retreat.

After pausing to take in the nature around me, I decided to visit a natural pool close to the condo. My husband and I walked down the street to the trailhead, turned the corner, and continued along the path to the pool. The tension in my body released, and I found that I was grateful for the sun, the sky, and the trees. It was hot walking the mile and a half through the forest on this summer's day, but we were rewarded by the river and a deep, natural pool of clear, cold flowing water. The water had made its way over these granite slabs over many years, creating a deep cavity as it continued downhill. You could literally slide into the pool because the stone was so worn from the water. As I made my way in, the water was bracingly cold, and it created a slight lapping against my body. On either side of the river were towering trees standing guard with the wind gently rustling the leaves, sounding like a whisper. I felt held by the earth.

The Buddha encouraged his disciples to meditate in the forest at the foot of a tree. That's also where the Buddha found enlightenment, referring to the Earth as his witness as he did. He took his son, Rahula, deep into the forest so that Rahula could be less concerned about daily life and his sense of self and more receptive to his father's teachings and the natural world around him.

I felt like Rahula that day in the pool. Not wrapped up in what had happened, but receptive to the beauty and support that surrounded me. Once again, nature reassured me that I was okay and that no matter what arose in my life, there are always sounds in nature to listen to, a forest to wander in, and a tree to sit under.

That night, as I lay in bed with the window open, a grey tree frog, a small, two-inch being, was extremely raucous and persistent in his mating calls. Despite the noisiness of his calls, I found his trill melodious and comforting. He continued his seeking late into the night and, in doing so, serenaded me until I fell into a deep and restful sleep.

3% UNCERTAINTY

When I met with the surgeon to discuss the pathology report, he said that the tumor was a grade 2, stage 1B, about as good as you can get. He went on to explain that there was only 3% uncertainty that the tumor was not completely removed, and that was because the blood vessels to the tumor were blah, blah, blah. I didn't hear anything after that. My mind seemed to get stuck on the word uncertainty.

That's because we are biologically oriented towards the negative. As the psychologist and author Rick Hansen says, *"the brain is like Velcro for negative experiences but Teflon for positive ones."* He goes on to explain that when we lived on the savanna millions of years ago, our ancestors needed to avoid two kinds of mistakes. One was thinking that there is a tiger lurking in the bushes when really, everything is okay, and thinking that everything is okay when really there is a tiger lurking in the bushes. The first results in needless worry, but the second results in no more gene copies. We are designed to make the first mistake a thousand times to avoid making the second mistake even once.

I was definitely stuck in the "there's a tiger lurking in the bushes, when really everything is okay." I was in the midst of needless worry, completely caught up in the what-ifs, oh no's, etc. When I got to my car, I took a moment to notice how my body felt… tight, constricted, and overwhelmed. I took a couple of deep breaths to create a bit of space around my thoughts and to allow my body to calm down. I got grounded by feeling my feet on the floor of the car, my butt in the seat, and my hands in my lap. Then I remembered to ask myself what I was accomplishing by thinking in this manner. I realized I was creating needless suffering for myself. I decided to look at the other statistic, which was that I was 97% fine! I could now focus on how grateful I was that I didn't need any further treatment. I'm not sure if I'll ever have any other issues related to this tumor, but worrying about it was creating more distress for me and putting me back into the "there's a tiger lurking in the bushes, when really everything is okay" mindset. I now understand that just because I am wired to notice the negative, doesn't mean I must let that wiring determine how I experience my life. I have a choice. And I choose to focus on the 97% certainty rather than the 3% uncertainty.

BELONGING

Wanting to belong is innate in our species. The feeling of not belonging is endemic in our culture.

I always felt like I didn't belong. It started in first grade when the boys used to call me Priscilla-Gorilla. And it went downhill from there. Until I figured out that I do belong and have always belonged. I recognized that my definition of belonging was too narrow; it was limited to that of wanting to fit in. And so, to be accepted and loved, I created a particular identity and sought accomplishments and possessions. But I still didn't feel like I belonged. Brené Brown says, *"I feel I belong everywhere I go, no matter where it is or who I'm with, as long as I never betray myself. And the minute I become who you want me to be in order to fit in and make sure people like me, is the moment I no longer belong anywhere."*

In early adulthood and for the first time in my life, I was accepted into the "cool" group. I was initially thrilled to be part of this social, fun cadre of women. But with time, what I found was that because I wanted to fit in so much, I changed who I was. I gave up my individuality. I was so disappointed to find out that to be part of this group, everyone had to follow one particular person's way of being; the way she looked, thought, ate, and even the television shows she watched. I fit into the group, but I did not feel like I belonged, nor did I want to.

Where did I belong, and what did that mean?

My sister, Stephanie, was sharing her frustration with the impossible-to-understand goings on at work. She felt like she was the only one who understood the scope and time requirements of the project she was managing, and her superiors kept pushing her to support an unrealistic timeline. She was agitated and discouraged at the inability of her superiors to explain what was true to their higher-ups. And she kept trying to explain to them again and again that their timeline wasn't going to work, and if they continued in this way, errors would naturally occur that would add to the cost of the project. After she said this, she paused, threw her head back, and exclaimed, "No one is listening to me!" As she did, we both started laughing at the ridiculousness of the situation. Our laughter released the tension in our hearts and minds, allowing us to acknowledge what was true by supporting each other in our understanding and care. This is the pleasant feeling of belonging.

I needed to get a replacement for my E-ZPass at the Rhode Island Turnpike and Bridge Authority. There is only one office in Rhode Island, and it usually has a long line of customers waiting for service. I took my place in line with everyone else on a beautiful spring day. As we waited and the line got longer and longer, those individuals who decided to stay started chatting. We weren't happy about the wait, but we made the best of it. It was joyful to be with a group of strangers who shared, laughed, and supported each other as we waited. I realized I felt so much a part of humanity in a way that I hadn't since before the pandemic.

It's so common to feel isolated and disconnected. From loved ones, friends, community, nature, and even ourselves. Electronic devices, such as phones, televisions, and video games, have become essential but are a poor substitute for the calming and nurturing reassurance we get from personal connections and nature, whether it's with our siblings, an acquaintance, or the trees that surround us. When we get jazzed up by our devices and the social media available online, making us anxious, it's important to take a break from them and re-experience the warmth and subtle interactions of being together with people and the natural world.

I felt like I belonged at Spirit Rock, a retreat center about an hour north of San Francisco. The meditation hall features high ceilings and large windows, letting the light in and giving us a view of the surrounding hills, grasses, trees, and wildlife. The space is quiet except for an occasional cough or sneeze. Sitting here, in silence, with one hundred other practitioners, I felt a profound sense of connection to both the place and the community.

At home, that pleasant feeling of belonging arises in me when the sun comes up early in the morning and my senses awake to the bright sunshine and cool breeze coming in through the window. Outside, I am aware of the smell of the ocean, or dirt, leaves, or burning wood, depending on the season. I am embodied with a feeling of being grounded, connected to the earth and every-thing around me. Being in the present moment, calm and curious. Cognitively, I know that I am part of the natural world, but it is not a cognitive process. I love this place of ease, relationship, and peace.

I often see a red-tailed hawk sitting on one of the branches of a maple tree in the yard, observing. She is stunning with warm brown feathers, a white underbelly, and a cinnamon-colored tail. She and her partner are longtime residents of this area, and it brings me joy to see her. But as I blink, she swoops down and grabs a baby rabbit scurrying in the lower field. I feel the contents of my stomach lift, shift, and then settle. And I understand that this, too, is nature. This is part of my belonging. Being present and connected to the nature that I am. My inseparability from life itself.

Buddhism suggests that by acknowledging and understanding the true nature of our existence, we can realize that we are not separate from but connected to each other and nature in ways that are subtle and not so subtle. Our mistaken belief in a permanent, separate self contributes to feelings of loneliness that are so pervasive now. For ancient philosophers of many Greek and Eastern schools, nature is understood as a process of life, of which human beings are an immanent part. And when we experience the natural world, we recognize we are not the center of the universe.

You and I are connected in this way and in others. We are also linked by the words put down on this page. Simply by my having written this and your reading of it, we are connected and belong to each other.

GRATITUDE

EACH MORNING WHEN I WAKE UP, I TAKE STOCK. How am I in this moment? This morning, I woke up irritated. Wow, that was unexpected! Rather than focusing on the story around why I was irritated, I observed the physical sensations in my body associated with "irritation," such as constriction and heaviness. Not so great. I didn't push it away, but allowed it to be part of my experience, and chose to bring my attention to a few things I was grateful for. I was grateful for the sunny day, that I felt well, and that I had time for a quiet cup of coffee.

The practice of gratitude gives us the biggest bang for our buck. A few minutes once or twice a day allows the possibility of shifting our attitude from an unwholesome to a wholesome mind state. By being aware of our thoughts and feelings, we can choose where we want our attention to be, making gratitude more accessible. This can incline the mind to thoughts of joy, curiosity, and appreciation rather than blame, negativity, and despair. The intention is to minimize the deepening of the neural pathways of the brain that create our habitual patterns of unhelpful thoughts and replace them with the possibility of more helpful thoughts.

My husband and I were hiking on a cold January day, midweek, up a familiar, snowy trail that, for some reason, felt especially challenging for me. As I struggled, I kept getting caught up in the "why is this so difficult?"

And then I heard a voice. I looked behind me, and moving quickly up the trail was a tall person with colorful, harlequin tights, a sweatshirt with the hood up, and a huge backpack. He greeted me with a big hello and a thanks for tamping down the snow on the trail so he could hike up it so quickly. I told him I couldn't take credit; it was those before me that had done the work. As he scooted by me, he replied, "Then thanks to the community of hikers who did it. I so appreciate them making it easier for me."

His unique attire and appreciation for the well-trodden path encouraged me to let go of the "why is this so difficult" and instead, reflect with gratitude on the blue sky, my physical strength, and the conservation of natural landscapes.

If you pause for a moment, what three things could you name that you are grateful for?

INSIGHT

Meditation is an activity that is thousands of years old and can be found in all spiritual traditions. In each tradition, it is supported by values such as compassion, patience, generosity, mindfulness, and wisdom. Much of what people are exposed to today is a simplified version of meditation, stripped of its context, ethics, and intention, monetized, and often misunderstood. Misunderstood because many people think that if they do meditation, all their problems will disappear. Or that they will at least find everlasting peace and calm.

With mindfulness or Vipassana meditation, that's not always the case. The cultivation of calm has many benefits and is supportive of the practice, but it is not the endgame. Insight is.

In the Buddhist tradition, insight is thought of as an understanding of the Four Noble Truths, a roadmap that describes the nature of suffering and how to end it. I like to think of insight as simply seeing things as they are, without bias, judgment, or opinion. For me, insight often occurs spontaneously and feels like a veil is lifted, showing me the truth of what is. There is also a felt sense that accompanies it. A feeling of yes, this is a truth I can feel in my bones, even if I haven't seen it clearly before.

One particular insight that came to me was around the concept of trust. I've always struggled with it. I set out again and again to "trust the world" and those in it. After having been burnt numerous times, I changed my strategy and tried to identify those that were "trustworthy."

I still made the wrong choices.

I reflected on several of these choices recently, where I trusted and was surprised that I shouldn't have. As I sat and reviewed these experiences with interest, curiosity, and without reactivity, what arose was that I was misplacing my trust. Where I needed to put that trust was in myself. Not in anyone else. Trust that I can navigate any situation that might arise. Trust that if I interact with someone untrustworthy, that would make itself known, and I could pivot to more skillful thoughts and actions. Trust in my own inherent goodness.

As this unfolded, I felt like a veil was lifted. I went from *I can't trust* to *I have a deep trust in myself.* Although this seems obvious as I read it, it was a profound shift for me. An ah-ha moment. I let go of an old habit of heart and mind that wasn't serving me. I literally gained a sense of freedom as this insight arose. And I felt like I could trust it.

2

RETREAT

Don't just do something, sit there!
                    —Sylvia Boorstein

MY FIRST RETREAT

The retreat wasn't what I expected.

When I got to the meditation center, I was given a room assignment, a yogi job, and a schedule for the retreat. It was February in Barre, Massachusetts, and it was cold in my room, so I turned the radiators on and headed to the retreat hall where we would officially begin. One hundred of us began the retreat by moving into silence. We then listened to a talk from one of the teachers. The talk was about metta, which I found out meant loving-kindness and would be the theme for the week. We did a metta meditation, and then I headed to bed. My roommate had not yet arrived.

I had no prior retreat experience. I was only here because this eight-day retreat fulfilled a prerequisite for the Mindfulness Yoga and Meditation Training program I would be attending later in the year.

The next morning, I noticed it was still chilly in my room. Brrr…. I checked to make sure the radiators were on, which they were, but it was only fifty-five degrees in the room. *Why wasn't it warmer? What's wrong with the heat?* I was so irritated. Not a good way to start the retreat.

I headed to the 5:30 a.m. sit in the hall and got myself settled on my cushion on the floor, closed my eyes, and struggled during the meditation. I was restless and easily distracted. I noticed that the person behind me was sniffling. Shouldn't she be in her room or in another meditation space so she wouldn't spread her germs? *How inconsiderate!* I was so angry. Finally, the teacher rang the bell, indicating the end of the forty-five-minute sit and the beginning of walking meditation.

During walking meditation, I went back to my room to see if it was any warmer and found my roommate in bed, sleeping. *Geez. It was the first day of the retreat, and she wasn't even going to go to the meditation hall. Why even bother to come to the retreat center if she was going to sleep the time away?* Now I was exasperated and judgmental.

Eventually, it was time for lunch. My yogi job was to wash pots, so I hurried to finish my lunch so I would make it to the kitchen on time. Not very conducive to mindfulness to have me hurry through lunch! I was aggravated that I couldn't mindfully enjoy my meal.

When I walked into the kitchen, I found the biggest pile of pots and pans I had ever seen. I was assigned pot drying and began as soon as my workmate finished washing her pot. She washed the pot very carefully, very mindfully, and *very* slowly. I couldn't help but think we would be here until tomorrow if she didn't *hurry up*. *Hurry up* my mind kept yelling. We won't make it to the next meditation if you don't *hurry up*.

She didn't.

So, for the next forty-five minutes, I bounced from thinking I am just going to jump in and help her wash the pots, to telling her to hurry up, to getting ready to scream. Five minutes before the next sit, the kitchen staff told us to go to the meditation hall and they would finish up. I wish I had known that before we started because I had gotten myself into a twit. I was upset that there wasn't clarity around the yogi job.

During the sit, I found I was still restless and uncomfortable, and my butt was getting sore. We had a break in the late afternoon, so I went for a long walk around the neighborhood so I could get rid of some of the energy and irritation that had built up. Between my room being cold, my roommate sleeping through the day, the sick retreatant, the pots not being done, and my sore butt, I wasn't happy. Actually, I was very upset. This retreat was not what I expected.

I started on my walk, and as soon as I did, I noticed that I was not paying attention to my surroundings, but I was caught up in a story in my mind. I realized it was a story that I created to soothe myself when I was upset. It was a story where I fixed all the things that I perceived were wrong around me. It was familiar, and yet, it was the first time I really noticed it.

When I returned to the retreat center, we did a few more sitting and walking meditations, had dinner, and ended the day with a talk from another one of the teachers. She expanded on this concept of metta by encouraging us to cultivate loving kindness, compassion, and care for ourselves. As we sat in our last meditation of the day, I paid more attention to the instructions the teachers gave us on using a metta phrase to allow this befriending toward oneself and others. I used the classic phrases "*May I be safe. May I be happy. May I be healthy. May I live with ease,*" trying to notice what arose with each phrase.

What I noticed was resistance, curiosity, muscle tightness, wanting, and quiet. So much to observe….

Then the bell rang. Whew! I realized I was exhausted! And irritated. And impatient. And sore. And this was only the first full day of the retreat!

But then over the next few days, I felt a subtle shift happening. The more I practiced metta, the less irritated I became. The room was still cold, but I spent so little time there that I didn't really mind. My roommate finally started attending the meditations, and that made me happy. The sniffling retreatant continued sniffling, and so I sent her some metta because I knew she was suffering. All of the pot washers got into a routine, and I just went with the flow that was established by my fellow retreatants. And most importantly, I found some compassion for myself. For the stories I told myself to self-soothe and comfort myself.

When we came out of silence at the end of the retreat, I learned a few things. One was that my radiator was broken. And my roommate, who had come from Europe, was overworked, had gotten a cold, and missed her flight to the States. I also found out that the sniffling retreatant wasn't sniffling, she was crying. She was crying because she had lost her husband recently and was mourning his death.

With this information, I reflected on my experience during the previous eight days. I realized I was judgmental, impatient, and irritated by everything I perceived was happening on the first day of the retreat. But with the practice of kindness towards myself and others, my heart opened, and I found more compassion and less judgment. I drove home with a different perspective and the skills to continue to cultivate this attribute called metta.

The retreat wasn't what I expected.

BELL RINGERS

I WAS ON A ONE-MONTH RETREAT IN NORTHERN California. I finally got into the flow of the daily routine, which consisted of eight hours of sitting practice interspersed with forty-five-minute periods of walking practice, an hour of work to support the community (cutting vegetables, cleaning pots and dishes, cleaning toilets, or vacuuming), and a bit of time to rest and complete activities of daily living. On retreat, we set aside our watches and cell phones to decrease distractions, so to notify the retreatants that it's time to go into the meditation hall, a bell is rung. And this is no ordinary bell.

Situated outdoors near the hall and covered in a rusty patina, the bell is about four feet long, round, and elongated, with a good-sized clapper or bell hammer. A crossbar holds it about eight feet off the ground near the meditation hall, so that no matter where you are, you can hear it. Designated bell ringers ring the bell at assigned times during the day.

I would often sit outside the meditation hall near the

bell waiting to go into the hall. The grounds are quite beautiful, and where I sat afforded me views into the valley and up towards the steep ridges and peaks that are part of the Pacific Coast Ranges Mountain system. But as I sat there each day, I became more drawn to the bell ringers and how they approached their task.

It seemed simple enough. The bell ringer goes to the bell and hits it. Perfunctory. Done. One of the bell ringers exemplified this. He approached the bell in a brisk, business-like fashion, grasped the bell hammer, held his breath, set his jaw, hauled back, and whacked the bell as hard as he could. The sound reverberated throughout the valley. Even before the bell stopped ringing, he replaced the clapper and was walking away. Ring bell … task done.

But watching other bell ringers made me realize that there are many ways to ring the bell. One yogi meandered up to the bell and observed it, taking in all aspects of it each time he drew near it…as if he were greeting it for the first time. And then and only then, he would take the hammer and gently brush it against the bell, perhaps to see what it was capable of in that moment. As if he were tuning an instrument, getting ready to fuse with it to create music. When he rang the bell, he did so with great ease and very little effort, as if the bell wanted to ring itself because of the care and concern he had shown it. The peal of the bell reverberated throughout the valley. He paused to be with the sound of the bell until it was done and gently returned the hammer. This was not a task completed. This was a person who had intention and was fully present for the experience of ringing the bell.

Both bellringers completed their task. But, for me, the experience was completely different between the two of them. When I noticed how I responded to the first bell ringer, I noticed agitation and impatience to get into the hall, and found that many of my muscles were contracted. I, too, was holding my breath and clenching my jaw. But when the second bell ringer approached the bell, I noticed a deep calm, curiosity, and expansion of my body. The second bell ringer brought to the moment full presence, awareness, and a connection to the bell. It is many years later, but I still think of him whenever I ring my small bells at the end of a sitting practice.

We all perform so many tasks each day, and we always have a choice of which bell ringer we want to be. I brush my teeth, take a shower, eat, drink, drive, and it is so easy not to be present for any of them. Why bother? It's the same old, same old, again and again. I do them and check them off as if my goal was to get to the end of the day. Perfunctory. Done. But in doing so, I miss the simple joy of being alive, of being aware and connected to my life.

Which bell ringer will I be today?

WALKING MEDITATION

LIFTING, MOVING, PLACING.... LIFTING, MOVING, placing....lifffttting, moooooving, plaaaaacccing.

These are the words I use to occupy my mind when I slow down my pace to do walking meditation so that I don't get carried off by my thoughts. Engaging the mind in this way is supposed to be helpful while mindful walking. Except it's not my mind that's the problem right now, it's my body. I just sat for forty-five minutes in meditation, and my body is so wound up that I think I'm going to explode. So, rather than following the traditional instructions of walking meditation, I take a cue from another yogi at this one-month retreat. He doesn't find a short path of ten to twenty feet and walks very slowly with full attention on the feet until the end of the path. There, we are told to note where the attention is and then turn to continue on that same path, maintaining the deep concentration developed in the hall to strengthen the mind/body connection. Instead, he's almost sprinting up and down the hill from the meditation hall to the dining hall, which is about the length of a football field and a twenty percent incline. And in doing so, he gives me permission to do the same. Hallelujah! Can one say that at a Buddhist retreat?

As I reflect on my practice of walking meditation, I accept that I don't do this practice as prescribed. I've tried. I'm averse to walking meditation; my favorite hindrance is restlessness, and I'm a rebel, so I'm not surprised that this is the case. Accepting this has allowed me to do what I need to do to best care for myself at the retreat. Like going down to the meditation hall to get a cup of tea instead of walking. Like increasing the pace and distance while walking. Like walking in a circle, noticing the leaning toward the inside of the circle, and then changing direction so that my leaning is consistent on both sides. And I still maintain the concentration cultivated in the hall.

Instead of doing the slow meditative walking as prescribed, at this retreat, I take advantage of the trails on the 411 acres in the hills of California. Whenever I can get a full hour, I hike into the hills and am mindful. I'm mindful of the path and pace, the effort it takes to get to the top of the hill so that I can take the trail to the other end and descend, creating a circle. I can see the Golden Gate Bridge in the distance at the high point of the trail, the deer eating nearby, and other yogis enjoying the outdoors and the views. I can feel the wind and sun on my face and notice when my breath increases as I go slowly uphill and how I need to engage different muscles in my legs and core so that I don't slide down the dirt path on the downhill. I'm focused, joyful, and in the moment.

After my "once around" is complete, I can feel the difference in my body. Calmer, more inclined to stillness and ease, and ready to sit for another forty-five minutes in the meditation hall. Until it's time again for another period of walking meditation.

DARK NIGHT OF THE SOUL

I WAS ALWAYS BEHIND. NO MATTER WHAT I DID, I couldn't catch up. And as I fell further and further behind, what I noticed was that my workmate hovered over me with a rigid stance and peered over at me with what felt like impatience, disdain, and disgust. Just like my mother used to do.

My yogi job at this one-month retreat was washing the dishes after the evening meal. The dishes were first wiped down and hand-washed by the retreatants, and then my workmate and I would stack them into the sanitizer, pull the dishes out at the end of the cycle, dry them, and put them away.

On the retreat's first evening, the two of us were shown what to do. The tasks were not difficult, but what we found that first evening was that no matter how we divided the tasks up, there were always lag times, and one of us would be ahead or behind. We finally agreed upon a way to divvy up the work so we could be both efficient and maintain the silence of the retreat. Yet, it seemed like I was the one always behind in my tasks.

During the ensuing days, the disdain and disgust that I felt from my workmate intensified, but it was also familiar and uncomfortable. I felt like he was judging me the same way my mother did when I was a child. And what was weirder was that he was German, just like my mother.

Later that week, I had my first meeting with my dharma teacher. Retreatants met with teachers twice weekly so that the teachers could help us navigate our way through a month of silence, meditation practice, meals, and our yogi job. I told him about my experience.

He listened and asked what I needed. I didn't know. He suggested I continue to notice and approach each evening with curiosity. I tried, but over time, the approach of work would trigger in me the same, increasingly escalating reaction so that just before I entered the kitchen, my heart rate was elevated, I was sweating, and starting to panic.

I was reliving my childhood. I thought I had dealt with all this stuff in therapy, but it all came rushing back. I no longer knew what was real and what wasn't, but after two weeks, somewhere in my soul or mind or heart, I decided I was done with the relentless suffering of reliving my past. Night after night, I would anticipate, judge, react, and suffer until I couldn't anymore. My body was done, my mind was done, and I was going to end this.

I didn't know how, but I knew I needed to talk to my teacher. I don't remember what I said when we met, but the bottom line was that I was done, and I was going back to my room to "release." Somehow, he trusted me on this, but he wanted me to check in later that evening with him.

I made no conscious decision for what followed, but walked into my room, lay on the bed, and writhed and writhed and writhed. It was accompanied by deep sobbing and whining. At the same time, I observed myself without reaction, thinking, "Good thing everyone is in the meditation hall because with these poorly built buildings, they'd be able to hear me all the way to the parking area!" I also vividly remember thinking, "This writhing is just like the shamanic releasing that I've read about to rid oneself of emotional trauma."

I don't know how long this lasted, but I was spent. I fell asleep, and when I woke up, I noticed the time. It was hours after my earlier appointment with my teacher, and I barely made it for my follow-up. I was a bit embarrassed when I told him what had happened, but he assured me that what I had gone through was not unusual; he had seen it before.

That evening, at my yogi job, I realized that I didn't much care for my workmate, but I no longer suffered from the fear and panic that had gripped me on previous evenings. That doesn't mean the feeling never arose again in my life, but it no longer defined my life in the same way because something had shifted. I had awareness, understanding, and compassion for this suffering and could face it no matter where or when it might show up.

In spiritual circles, this type of event is sometimes noted as the "dark night of the soul" or a "period of difficulty on the contemplative path that can result in insight." Scientific research on meditation might describe it as an "adverse event" or, in Buddhist texts, as "meditation sickness" or simply that causes and conditions came together in a particular way. I think that the universe conspired to put me in the exact place I needed to be with the care and support that was necessary so that I could face and move through some very old and very deeply ingrained traumatic memories. Whatever it was, I am deeply grateful.

SAVING THE DAY

It was winter, and I was on retreat in Massachusetts. I had been there for a few days and was taking a walk around the neighborhood. I felt the cold air and noticed that the rhythm of walking settled my body and mind. As I paid attention to what was around me, I could appreciate the outline of the trees against the sky, the warmth of my torso as I walked, and the coolness of the air on my face. What I also noticed was what my mind was thinking. I was seeing it the same way I was seeing the trees, from a distance and with interest.

What I saw was a particular story. And it went something like this. Someone did something that made me feel bad or insecure. Perhaps it was a slight or a mean remark. I was thinking about a family member who had raised their voice to me and said a few things in a way that made me feel uncomfortable; I felt like I needed to defend myself. It was accompanied by heavier breathing, hunched shoulders, and a desire to act out.

It was as if someone was reading this story to me, and

the plot started to thicken. I was getting anxious and a bit fearful, and viewed the family member as wrong, and I was going to fix it and them. I was going to teach them a lesson and, in the process, I would be the hero of my story. And then I would feel safe and secure. Which is what I desperately needed.

Multiple variations of this story came up during the retreat. I knew because I felt vulnerable and insecure whenever it showed up. But the truth was that I was safe at this retreat center in the woods. This way of thinking was happening all on its own and not at all reflective of what was happening in the moment.

After leaving the retreat and returning home, I continued to pay attention to this story. I noticed when it was there and when it wasn't. I started to notice what led to the arising of the story. I knew why I told this story to myself; it was a habitual response to an old wound. But knowing that didn't help. It was still accompanied by anxiety and fear. And a strong compulsion to stay in the story until I felt better…safer.

A teacher suggested I treat the story like an old friend. Someone who was familiar to me so that I could turn towards it and be with it a little more easily. I decided instead to treat it like a relative I didn't like but needed to interact with. That was more realistic. As time went on, the story still came up, but being with it in this way started to change my relationship to it. I realized it was simply trying to protect me and that it was a strategy that a young child came up with in a difficult situation. I started to extend some compassion to it and myself as I understood its intention. And with that compassion, it started to soften, and I was able to hold it with some spaciousness even though it was still there. As the spaciousness grew, there were other things that were held there: warmth, curiosity, and a variety of memories.

One of the memories was a cartoon from my childhood. It was a silly cartoon about a mouse called Mighty Mouse who was fashioned after Superman and had many of the same superpowers. Each episode consisted of a crisis that required extraordinary help to resolve, and Mighty Mouse would use his superpowers to come to the aid of the person needing it. When Mighty Mouse was on the way to right some type of wrong, he would sing, "*Here I come to save the day.*" It was a foolish little jingle that seemed to be etched in my mind and brought a smile to my face.

I started to sing, "*Here I come to save the day,*" to myself each time my hero story arose, and a funny thing happened. I wasn't caught up in the story anymore. It seemed to cut through the emotional attachment I had with it and brought me back to this present moment. Being present in the moment, I understood that I was just fine. And although both the discomfort and the story didn't go away, whenever I used the jingle, I felt like I gained some space from it. I was now seeing the story the same way as I was seeing the trees on my walk, from a distance and with interest.

SHAME

In my thirties, I got involved in a project evaluating the care and services available for the elderly in Rhode Island. It was an initiative funded by a local businessman interested in politics and policy development in healthcare. I was the only female and a volunteer on this board: a small cadre of well-known individuals. At a meeting, I offered an example of how to care for those with dementia and Alzheimer's that was being modeled in one of the senior centers in the state, but it was not well-received because it was introduced by a nurse without the proper research behind it. My nursing experience saw the value of it. But after I offered my suggestion, there was a long pause, and it seemed to me that the head of the group turned up his nose, everyone looked at each other without saying anything, and then we moved on to a different topic. I was always terrified of making mistakes, and I felt like I just made one. I felt shame.

Whether it was being called out for not including a

child with physical limitations on my running team at age eight, answering the question with the wrong answer in class at age ten, having a "friend" tell the guy we were friends with that I had a crush on him at fourteen or getting fired from the roadside deli at sixteen, my response was always the same. It was shame.

Shame is defined as a painful feeling of humiliation or distress caused by the consciousness of wrong or foolish behavior. And I so often thought my behavior was wrong or foolish, and therefore, I often felt shame. It accompanied me everywhere.

*

The meditation hall is a large, open space with incredibly high ceilings and windows that allow the beauty of the outside in. The wood floors and walls give it a warm glow, and the dais is simple and serene. We are all trying to sit still and upright, whether it is in a chair or on a cushion on the floor. The room is enveloped in silence, as it always is in the hall, and we are waiting for the teacher to begin their evening talk.

Pascal is the teacher tonight, and he begins with a funny story about when he was on retreat many years ago. Sitting on the floor during one of the meditations, he noticed that any sneeze, cough, or rare noise occurring in the hall seemed extraordinarily loud and irritating. He knew that his heightened response to the sounds was due to the intensity of this particular retreat and the deep levels of concentration he attained. But when a fellow retreatant sneezed multiple times, it sent him over the edge. Because his sense of hearing was so sensitized, he couldn't tolerate being in the hall any longer and thought it best to leave. But because he was so distressed about the noise, he didn't notice that his legs had fallen asleep, and as he got up, he fell forward onto the dais with a big thud! His head was sideways, facing the teacher, and when she asked him if he was okay, he shouted, "It's too loud!" When the teacher asked the other retreatants if it was too loud in the hall, he could see that they all shook their heads no.

All of us erupted into laughter and rolled around on our cushions and chairs as Pascal told his story. But as I listened to his story and joined in the laughter, I had an interesting response. I felt shame.

Somewhere deep inside me, a voice said, "He should have been mortified!" I knew that this voice was reflecting what I would have felt in that situation. I knew that not only would I have left the hall in shame, but I would have also immediately left the retreat, and never, ever returned.

But then another inner voice replied, "But he wasn't mortified, and he even shared his story with a hundred people *and* made it funny! If he wasn't feeling shame, why should I?" And the shame went away.

Shame made itself known again later in the retreat.

Again, Pascal was giving a talk, this time about the Four Noble Truths, which is a foundational teaching well known to him and the retreatants. But something happened. He started his talk, but it didn't make any sense. He was all over the place. I felt like he was making a fool of himself. I was embarrassed for him.

After a while, he paused, looked at the retreatants, and said, "This isn't going well, but I'm going to continue and see what happens."

What?

He very calmly acknowledged what was true without hiding it, compensating for it, or showing any fear or shame. Again, "If he wasn't feeling shame, why should I?"

The depth of my shame became evident at this retreat, but so did the understanding that shame is an optional response. The shame I felt wasn't necessary or true. I had been shown that twice, and I realized that it was not the actions that were shameful, but my reactions, my feelings of being inadequate and unworthy. And in reflecting on the cause, I knew that the neglect and emotionally distant parenting of my childhood created the shame. But that was many years ago, and I know now that I am adequate and worthy. And now, rather than fall into that same old reflexive trap, I recognize when shame arises, and I simply say, "If he wasn't feeling shame, why should I?"

LOST MY GREEN

WE ALL BROUGHT OBJECTS TO THE RETREAT CEN-
ter that represented different aspects of our histories,
beliefs, and desires. A variety of beautiful things were
offered and placed on the altar; a funeral brochure of
someone's dad who had passed away just two weeks
earlier, to a small musical instrument celebrating that
person's career.

But the item that really caught my attention was an
aspen leaf. The woman who offered it described the life
cycle of the aspen leaf and correlated it with her own...
a small bud that grew until it unfurled and showed itself,
open and light green. Then, being part of the community
and season, engaged and in the prime of her life, the leaf
evolved to a darker green.

But when she offered the aspen leaf, it wasn't green.
She had picked it off the tree specifically because it had
lost its green, just like her. Usually, aspens turn yellow,
but this one was a combination of brilliant orange and
red. And although beautiful, she acknowledged that as it

continued to change in color, the leaf would eventually fall off the tree, wither, and die.

We are about the same age, the woman and I, and I recognized that I, too, had lost my green. Green, synonymous with that season of harmony and growth, of raising families, expanding careers, and cultivating friendships, had gone. Now, often relegated to being invisible, thought of as frail and perhaps a bit slow or senile, I realized that these shifts reflect our society and its view on aging, although I do not see myself in that way. Many Eastern cultures revere their elders, recognizing their wisdom. In Native American cultures, old age brings respect and leadership. Other traditions designate this time in life as an opportunity to "go forth," when a layperson leaves home to follow the spiritual life.

Western society does not share these perspectives.

Despite Western society's view, this woman spoke about her own personal intention of celebrating this beautiful season of color and richness. She had finally slowed down, able to enjoy friends and family and observe life in a way she had not had the opportunity to do until now.

Aspen trees are known for their resilience and interconnected root systems, and we can use that imagery at any age to help us embrace change and cultivate new opportunities. The aspen's quaking leaves symbolize awareness and presence. And if you look up what red and orange symbolize, they are reflections of strength and optimism, respectively. Although we had both lost our green, we both smiled as we recognized our own resilience and saw this time in our lives as an opportunity for more depth and connection. We will continue to move through our transitions, as we all must, anticipating our next color change, not with regret but with the awareness and presence of an aspen leaf.

DEATH

THEY STOOD TALL AND STRAIGHT IN THE DIS-
tance, crowded, in different shades of green. When I sat
and meditated outdoors at this retreat center, these trees,
mostly ponderosa pine and aspen, made up my entire
view, from left to right. But as the land drew closer to
the river and then to me, it transitioned from forest into
meadow. At that intersection, one tree stood out. It was
incredibly tall with a perfectly straight trunk, a spine
that lifted it into the heavens. But it was quite different
from the others.

It was dead.

Although its trunk was tall and straight, it had no pine
needles, and the branches it had left were shortened and
mangled, like arthritic fingers. It no longer had gnarly
bark, as all ponderosa pines do, which had fallen off, and
what was left was a monotone grey, except where it had
a deep, large wound that encompassed almost the entire
width of the trunk on the lower third of the tree. The
wound looked like the tree had been eviscerated, with

only a bit of its innards still intact. Those portions were shades of beige, grey, brown, and black, accenting what was left.

This ponderosa pine was beautiful in some strange way. It seemed vulnerable but also had a dignity that I can't describe. A dignity that defied its death.

Because it wasn't done yet.

It still had purpose.

It served as food for insects and the birds perched on its upper limbs, or what was left of them. And when the earth is finally ready to let it go to the ground, it will feed, house, and support fungi, mosses, lichens, invertebrates, birds, mammals, reptiles, and amphibians. The living and dead intertwined.

As I observed this tree in death and what it continued to offer our ecosystem, I began to wonder, what is death? In the West, death is treated as a bad thing, almost like a failure, so we hide it and sanitize it. We consider it "the end" where the body stops functioning and starts to decompose. But some people whose loved ones suffer from dementia or Alzheimer's say their loved ones are no longer here. Did they die before their bodies did?

Or will they die more than once? First, when they lost cognitive function, and then again when their bodies ceased functioning.

If we can sense those we have lost by bringing them to mind and feeling them by remembering their voice, smell, image, and memories together, are we keeping them "alive"? So, maybe they are not gone, maybe they just moved on.

I often call on a childhood friend who died in her thirties to send me some of her chutzpah when I am hesitant to move forward on something I find difficult. Her memory fills me with strength and joy, and she's been dead for over thirty years.

Or is she?

Some traditions say that you don't really die until your name is said for the last time. My nieces and nephews often speak about their grandfather, and all the wonderful times and adventures they had with him. And my father-in-law comes alive and is with us when they do.

Others say that we are a process and constantly transitioning to other forms of existence. This truly resonates with me. And it reflects what I saw in that tree. We come into existence as a human just as a ponderosa pine comes from a seed from one of its cones, a crap shoot of genes in both cases. Then we transition from an embryo, into an infant, maturing to a child, to an adolescent, to an adult, to an elder. We transition from healthy to sick, maybe back to healthy, and sometimes something in between. This process is as profound as the process of transitioning from a physical form to a non-physical form. Our bodies may decompose, but our deeds, interactions, and perhaps genes continue. Is this us or a form of us? Did we die, or is it yet another transition, another mutation?

The Buddha lives on in his teachings. He is as alive

today as he was more than 2600 years ago. His purpose in life was to alleviate suffering and the causes of suffering, and his teachings continue and nourish his legacy. The tree at the retreat center is also dead, but it lives on in the transitions it undertakes to give life to other plants and animals, and then by becoming the earth itself, nourishing her as a mother would nourish her child. Perhaps that is its most important purpose and contribution.

GOT MY ASS KICKED

At least once a year for fourteen consecutive years, I went on an in-person retreat. I would be there any time between a week and a month, which gave me the opportunity to be aware of and investigate more fully how my mind worked.

And then, in 2020, the pandemic happened. Everything shut down. First, we thought it would be for a few days, then a few weeks, but then things stayed shut down for months, and then for more than a year. In-person retreats moved online.

More than four years later, I was finally able to attend an in-person retreat. Meditating at home, I am mostly in maintenance mode, but retreat time is an opportunity for me to take a deeper dive. On retreat, I pay more attention to long-time habitual patterns and karmic knots. Whereas I am intermittently constricted around these patterns and knots at home, on retreat, they take on a different quality. They are more interesting than consuming, and with the spaciousness of retreat, these issues are more approachable, and I can be more accepting of them.

It usually takes me a day or two to get settled into the daily routine, and I do that by making sure I get enough sleep and overeat a bit, which grounds me. As I do meditation practice, I watch my mind eject tons of thoughts, concerns, and stories until it, too, is a bit more settled. This can result in ease and concentration.

Unfortunately, that's not what happened on this in-person retreat.

As soon as I closed my eyes, I was transported back home. There were a variety of difficult issues that had unfolded in the months prior to the retreat, and I didn't know how they would be resolved or even if they would. Each time I thought about one issue, I'd catch myself and then fall into thinking about the other issues. I was perseverating on the worst-case scenario in each instance. And then I noticed other things coming up. My habitual response to uncertainty and chaos. The karmic knot of anxiety. And then I just didn't feel well. This triggered even more anxiety because it reminded me that in the past, I would push myself so hard in my daily life that when I got to retreat, I'd be sick with a cold or some other illness that indicated that I was overdoing it.

This did not subside over the first three days. No matter where I went or what I did. Relentless thoughts, restlessness, and rumination. I was getting my ass kicked. I felt completely defeated.

I knew I needed support and perhaps to take a different tack. So, I took advantage of the optional meeting with the teachers to talk about what was coming up for me. I talked to the teacher about how I got caught up in wanting things to be a certain way. I noticed that as soon as I resisted what was present, I was in that place of anxiety and rumination.

With their direction, support, and most importantly, validation, I went from feeling defeated to knowing that even though these thoughts were powerful, they were just thoughts that were empty. Mind events that arise and fall away that exist due to causes and conditions. They are not substantial and influence me only if I let them. Some were not even true. I needed to once again be reminded of that.

Another strategy I employed was to use mindfulness tools that I was familiar with but had never utilized before, mostly because they just had never resonated with me.

But I was willing to try them now. Because we were practicing outside on land in northern New Mexico, which consisted of a combination of rugged landscapes, grasslands, and woodlands, the teachers invited us to meditate with our eyes open, which I don't usually do because the visual stimulation distracts me. But this time I found that I could stay in the present moment as

I scanned the rocky outcroppings, the colors of the trees, the ever-changing sky, the birds, and the movement of the grasses that were on the grounds.

And I've always disliked walking meditation, but I did quite a bit of it on this retreat. Walking along a short path among the wildflowers or along a short stretch of the river that abutted the retreat center felt more like a meandering than a formal practice. The repetition of my steps calmed my nervous system, as did the running stream and flora and fauna that surrounded me. My attitude slowly shifted from distress to gratitude.

With a twenty-year practice, I thought I knew all there was to know about being on retreat. I don't. Just like how we thought COVID would come and go, it didn't. Life unfolds in its own way and in its own time. Maybe next retreat I'll remember that so that I don't get my ass kicked.

WORD PLAY

Sampappalapa. Yes, this is a word. Not in English, but in Pali, the language spoken during the Buddha's lifetime. Pali isn't used anymore, but there are several scholars who have learned the language so that they can translate the earliest Buddhist texts. I am not a Pali scholar, but I have heard these words often during retreats where they are used to capture the essence of an idea or teaching.

I pay attention to these words because they are different and unusual. Also, they don't carry the baggage of a well-worn English word. For instance, metta METT-ah is sometimes translated from the Pali as loving-kindness. For many, the word love has a specific connotation and is understood in a particular and limited way. But Pali words can have various meanings dependent on the context in which they are used, which makes them rich and complex. So, metta can mean a wish for happiness, care, kindness, loving, benevolence, friendliness, amity, befriending, or goodwill towards ourselves or others.

There is even a metta practice that supports well-being and resilience, as well as being used as a concentration practice.

Back to sampappalapa. SAM-PAPPA-LA-PA. To me, sampappalapa sounds like gibberish, which is sort of what it means. It's translated to something like talking nonsensical, or useless or pointless speech. In other words, gossip, idle chatter, the act of talking just for the sake of talking. It even sort of sounds like blah, blah, blah, blah. There's an element of onomatopoeia in the word.

The other day, I had the experience of observing sampappalapa at the gym. I was in the women's locker room, and two women were talking to each other. Well, they were actually talking at each other. One began to speak, and the other interrupted her midsentence and started talking about a completely different topic. Then the other would reply before she was done, but then switch to talking about a friend of theirs in a not-so-complimentary fashion. And then she changed the subject again, not allowing her friend to respond to the previous topic. I couldn't keep track of it all and thought that this was just a bunch of jibberish… sampappalapa.

Papancha. PA-PAN-CHA. This word sounds like what it is as well… on and on and on and on or a different kind of blah, blah, blah. Where sampappalapa is verbal proliferation, papancha is often translated as mental proliferation. This term is used to describe the tendency of the mind to add onto our basic experience memory, opinions, and biases, creating waves of mental elaboration, most of which are illusory, repetitive, and even obsessive, preventing any sort of mental calm or clarity of mind. This habitual pattern always sends me down the rabbit hole of unhelpful stories and anxiety. Last night I had a variety of tasks to do and was tired. Instead of looking at what needed to be done and prioritizing, I thought about how I shouldn't take so much on, if I had only done some of this work yesterday, what was I thinking, I'll never get it done, I'll get charged a late fee, blah, blah, blah. You get the idea.

Ehipassiko. EH-HE-PAS-E-KO. At a retreat, a teacher gave a talk on noticing unwholesome states of mind, such as anger or blame, and how to work with them. At the end of his talk, he said, "Ehipassiko. Don't take my word for it, but try it out for yourself." Ehipassiko is often translated as "Come and see for yourself." Its intention is to encourage investigation. This inquiry allows us to discover our own truth, creating freedom and personal growth. We can be curious and examine our habitual patterns without judgment. For instance, if I become aware that I am having negative thoughts, the invitation is to investigate what it feels like in the body. Does it feel good? If not, is it worth my while to continue thinking these thoughts? Does it create harm for myself or others?

Mudita. MU-DEE-TA. Mudita describes a state of joy, one that embodies the pleasure that comes in delighting in another person's good fortune. It was the feeling I had when my friend's daughter got married in Italy, and when I heard that my nephew and his wife were expecting twins. I find the word amusing because when you say the second syllable, DEE, it forces you to smile, reflecting the state of happiness you can feel for another.

Mindfulness asks us to look at our experience with kindness and curiosity, offering us a variety of different methods to do so. Whether it is going on retreat, practicing meditations to cultivate concentration, or embracing a new vocabulary, mindfulness invites us to pay attention to what we do and how we do it.

But don't take my word for it. Ehipassiko… try it out for yourself and see what happens.

TEACHERS

Retreat is an extraordinary opportunity to practice with experienced and knowledgeable meditation teachers. On longer retreats, there are often multiple teachers to instruct and support the participants because being with oneself in silence allows layers of old patterns and protection to fall away. Retreatants can be relieved, surprised, scared, or confused about what shows up.

Many years ago, I attended a one-month retreat with five teachers responsible for assisting and encouraging me and the other ninety-nine retreatants. As we came to the end of the month, it was clear that there was tension among the teachers. One wasn't feeling well, another was short-tempered and raised her voice to one of the participants, and the others were somewhere in between. They no longer showed the united front they did at the beginning of the retreat.

Each day, a teacher shared their knowledge in an evening talk. They usually included a nugget of wisdom in these talks, but I realized that these teachers may or may not be wise themselves. Although they knew the topics well intellectually, the dissonance among them suggested to me that they didn't necessarily embody the wisdom they espoused.

I came to meditation practice thinking I could find the answers to my most profound questions outside myself, from the teachers, and in doing so, abdicated my own knowledge and wisdom. I regained them both at this retreat. What I learned was that these teachers were human. And I could learn from their humanness. I also learned that the real teachers and teachings that I needed to pay attention to were all around me. And I could lean into my own innate wisdom. The meditation master Ajahn Chah said "… *Wisdom is in you, just like the sweet, ripe mango is already in a young green one. With even a little intuitive wisdom, you will see the ways of the world. You will come to understand that everything in the world is your teacher.*"

After the one-month retreat, I was standing at the stove in my home, making dinner, and was deep in thought about an issue that had come up at work. My husband asked me a question and I replied curtly. He paused and then started to make comments that started to irritate me. Rather than respond in my usual snarky way, I paused and asked myself, "What's going on here? Is he goading me?" As I reflected on this, there wasn't any irritation or pushback on my part, just curiosity. So, I asked him if he was goading me. And to my surprise, he said yes. He said that I was too quiet for his comfort and that I had responded curtly, so he thought I was mad at him. And because of that, he wasn't sure how to interact with me. If he knew I was annoyed, that would be okay, and he felt comfortable giving me space or leaving the room. What I learned is that I don't often express my emotions to him, and I vowed that I would be more forthcoming. Over time, it has allayed his concerns and made me more open and aware of my emotional state and how it affects others.

Teaching moments happen frequently now, exposing my long-standing habitual patterns and aversive behaviors. If I can pay attention to them without reactivity as they arise, I can choose to respond in a way that is helpful to myself and to others. Another lesson learned.

IMPERMANENCE

EVERYTHING CHANGES.

As I read the essays that make up this book, I realize that they are simply a snapshot of who I am at a particular moment in time. They mark different points in my life from 2005 to 2025, and the insights, lessons, joys, and sorrows that I've experienced. Some experiences contradict others. They include people I know well, some I am no longer acquainted with, some I miss, and some I might occasionally see. There are many people who are important to me who are not featured in these essays, and I am a different person even from the one you read about in my most recent story.

Everything changes. Sometimes quickly and sometimes not so quickly, but we get fixated on the idea that change is a problem. Change is uncomfortable and makes us feel vulnerable and unsteady. But it's true, moment to moment. Whether it's knowing that every single one of the cells in our body turns over every seven years or that Mount Everest is growing in height, everything is changing. In addition, our emotions change, our thoughts change, and physical sensations change moment-to-moment. And that's the good news that we can take from knowing that everything changes because we don't need to get stuck in painful experiences.

Our human suffering is caused by our attachment to impermanent things, our sense of self, and the way we want things to be. We want to grab onto something safe, tangible, consistent, better, unchanging.

This realization came to me as I reflected on a series of retreats I attended at a specific retreat center. I've embraced this center for a variety of reasons; the weather is consistently pleasant, the land is spacious and beautiful, animals live freely on the preserved grounds, and the retreat center is private. These characteristics have been consistent over the years I have sat retreats there, but I noticed that I was resistant to any changes or "upgrades" that the center made.

I was resistant to the solar panels that were placed on the land near the hiking trails on one of my retreats. I felt like it marred the land.

The retreat center built a beautiful, large, new community center that replaced the old, rickety trailer that the locals used for gatherings, such as day-long retreats and evening sits. The old trailer was tucked into a small depression on the land under a canopy of trees at the retreat entrance. I felt the new community center took up too much open space and was too upscale.

The guiding teachers have changed; they are all much younger than I am. And some of the well-known teachers have died. Many stepped back years before they passed away, and I could feel my resistance to hearing of their decisions and deaths.

I recognized this wanting of the retreat center to stay exactly as I remembered it. But I was determined the last time I was there to be open to any changes that may have occurred. I hoped it would feel more like being in the flow of a river or riding an ebbing and flowing tide than the contracted grasping of wanting things to be stagnant, unchanged, or fixed.

I saw that the retreat schedule had changed with a later start time. I simply moved with the energy of the group as we went into and out of the meditation hall.

Some of my favorite hiking trails were closed due to the drenching rains California had just before arriving. I explored other trails I wasn't as familiar with or hadn't hiked on.

I sat with teachers I was unfamiliar with and much younger than I was. I noticed an energy and enthusiasm that was heart-warming.

The kitchen staff had completely turned over, and the meals were different but also delicious.

I also noticed that I settled into the retreat much more quickly than usual and felt more grounded rather than restless, as I so often did. And I found comfort in what was familiar: the upper meditation hall, the temperate climate, and the variety of animals. I will continue to go on retreat to this center as long as it is available and as long as I can. I feel grateful for every opportunity to be there. Because it all might change tomorrow. And I'm okay with that.

3

EVERYDAY LIFE

The miracle is not to walk on water. The miracle is to walk on earth. —Línjì Yìxuán

MY FIRST INSIGHT

Cultivating caring, mellow, objective, and equanimous states was often easy on retreat. Not so easy in my daily life. I had hoped to integrate and embody these states so they became traits, consistent and long-lasting, but when I returned home from retreats, I would revert back to the selfish, restless, intense, vigilant individual I was so familiar with.

Soon after attending a retreat, I was at my local yacht club, disagreeing with an older gentleman on the race committee about buying an automatic race start sequence horn. We planned to run a few regattas that year, and the horn would make it easier to get and retain race committee members. He strongly disagreed with me; he had many years of experience running regattas without one. His voice started to get louder and more insistent, and I thought he wasn't interested in exploring this new idea. As his voice started to get louder, I reacted; mentally, emotionally, and physically. And I could see it all happening. Clenching of my jaw, holding my breath, an increase in my heart rate, and resistance to compromise. I could also hear my voice getting louder, and I was getting more insistent, and I was aware of that, too. I wasn't proud of my actions, but at the time, I attributed my reaction to the subject matter and his resistance to the idea.

A week later, I was having a conversation with a younger woman who was helping me in my garden. She disagreed with my new garden design, and her voice started to get louder and more insistent, and I thought she wasn't interested in exploring this new idea. As her voice started to get louder, I reacted; mentally, emotionally, and physically. And I could see it all happening. Clenching of my jaw, holding my breath, an increase in my heart rate, and resistance to compromise. I could also hear my voice getting louder, and I was getting more insistent, and I was aware of that, too. I wasn't proud of my actions, but this time, in observing it, I saw the similarities between the two conversations. I realized that what triggered my reaction was the tone, insistence, resistance, and loudness of the voices in both situations. It was me reacting to old conditioning. I recognized it because I was paying attention not only to what was happening externally, but also internally. It was me and my reactivity and not the subject matter or any individual.

And although I could see this all clearly, I still reacted with defiance and a loud voice. It would take me months before this conditioning would lose its charge. And I couldn't force it. Awareness precedes all of it. I needed to observe and allow the emotions to rise and fall away on their own. With this insight, I was confident that with time and awareness, I'd cultivate those caring, mellow, objective, equanimous states so they would finally become traits.

FIVE WOMEN IN A JEEP

"When is the service for Mary?" Lisa asked.

Rene, Elizabeth, Rose, Lisa, and I were in a jeep heading into All Saints when we pulled over to ask John, who was pushing his bicycle up the hill, about the funeral service. Elizabeth, who had gathered us together for this vacation in Antigua, had spent many winters here and knew Lisa well. Lisa grew up in Antigua with her family heavily invested in its infrastructure. She seemed to know everyone on the island; John and Mary sang with her in her church choir.

Rene, Rose, and I had never been to Antigua. We were all older, white women connected by our relationship to Elizabeth as well as by our practices of yoga and meditation.

When Lisa pulled over to ask her friend John, who was native to the island, about the service, he greeted us warmly and then said, "We haven't scheduled it yet, but I'll let you know when we do."

He then paused, looked at each of us, one by one,

before taking in the scene as a whole and stated, "Five women in a jeep."

That was it.

He then said his goodbyes and pedaled away.

What was he thinking when he said that?

As I contemplated some of the possibilities, this is what came to me. The cumulative age of the women was 322. The oldest woman was driving the jeep. Each was some combination of daughter, sibling, parent, grandparent, or spouse. Lost were a spouse and a child. One had breasts missing, and another had no ovaries or uterus. All had worked and supported themselves as jewelers, business owners, nurses, massage therapists, artists, and land developers. Each had dealt with disappointment, unhappiness, betrayal, love, joy, and loss.

This was all true, but was it what John was thinking? Probably not, since he knew nothing of our histories. I had filled in my own not knowing with this lovely story that made me feel happy and proud.

Maybe John's comment related to the privilege he saw. Antigua had suffered with colonial racism since the English took over the island and enslaved its people. Antiguans were "freed" in 1833, although still very much oppressed. Then the Americans brought in a whole different level of racism when they established a base in Antigua in 1941. And here were these rich, privileged white women driving around like they owned the place. This too was true, but I again filled in the space of not knowing with another story, one that made me feel sad and guilty.

I was filling in that void of "I don't know" by layering onto John's comment my own thoughts, ideas, experiences, and biases… this is *papanca* or mental proliferation. More clearly understood as a view of the world created in the mind through language and concepts, which can cause suffering. And these stories were causing me suffering in that they affected my ability to see the experience clearly, as well as creating all types of emotions that had nothing to do with the actual encounter. Through these imposed narratives, I experienced the world through my mind's interpretation of it and not how it actually was, a view that often puts me at the center of things, whether we really are or not.

When I again paused to reflect on this, I realized that I didn't know what John was thinking when he made his comment, and I'd never know. So, what was it that I did know? Only that there was a man on a bicycle and five women in a jeep.

BLUEBERRY DELIGHT

My husband and I love being outdoors, and hiking gives us the opportunity to do it in all kinds of weather. It doesn't make any difference what season it is because things are always changing. Leaves morphing from red to yellow to orange, falling and then blooming again, the ever-modulating sound of the streams depending on how much water is flowing, strong to gentle breezes, deep snow or none, animal tracks, the coolness, or warmth of the air, the birds singing. I joyfully pay attention to all I see, hear, and feel when I am outdoors in nature.

This past weekend, my husband and I hiked one of our favorite trails in New Hampshire, beloved because of the occasional, large ledges interspersed among the acres of evergreens, offering beautiful views of the valley and beyond.

On this hike, we had to pay particular attention as we headed up the mountain. The previous day's rain had left the trail wet, muddy, and the rocks and ledges slippery.

The going was slow, requiring concentration with each step so that I wouldn't slip, lose my balance, or fall. I needed to be aware of the wetness of the roots and moss and the pitch of the incline to navigate safely. As the trail grew steeper and ledges more prevalent, my attention narrowed even more, now being with each individual movement. I was honing a fine balance between making sure my feet were solid and secure and dedicating my senses to what was just in front of me. Near the top of the mountain, I found a path along a ledge where there was some shrubbery and a few stunted trees to grab onto if necessary. As I walked along the edge, I noticed a shrub just beneath me. It was only about a foot tall but had numerous small berries. They were blueberries! Tons of blueberries!

"Hey, Louis!" I yelled to my husband. "I found a blueberry bush with lots of berries on it." He responded with "I found some, too. Come over here and we can sit and have some."

I made my way over and sat next to him. We were on a natural outcropping of rock, safe and comfortable, where we could look out onto the valley and the mountains that surrounded us. Under the bright sun accompanied by a few fluffy clouds, the breeze was just starting to pick up, helping us cool down from the effort we needed to engage in to hike up the mountain. And we were surrounded by small, vigorous shrubs that were heavily laden with blueberries that grew out of the cracks, nooks, and crannies of the mountain. Anywhere there was dirt.

I picked a couple of berries and put them in my mouth. As I bit into them, they exploded. Soft, sweet, and juicy. Perhaps the best blueberries I've ever had. I picked a few more and ate them as Louis and I shared our delight. I felt like a child who had found a treasure. We both smiled, and I felt so much joy! Sitting in the sun, looking out onto the valley on a beautiful day, eating wild blueberries with my husband.

And then it hit me. The *wanting*. The wanting of more than what was here, the desire, the craving…. *"Oh, these are such good blueberries. I'll pick a bunch and bring them home so we can have blueberries with breakfast in the morning. I have a plastic bag in my pack. But I'll need to carry them outside the pack, otherwise they'll get smashed. That's okay. I'll manage with my hiking poles and the berries. I could put the poles in my pack and just carry the berries. It's worth it. If I get a lot, I can make a blueberry sauce."* Strategizing, planning, wanting, and thinking about the future. I was now sitting in my kitchen getting ready to have breakfast with a plastic bag full of blueberries that didn't exist.

So, what is craving? In this case, it was an overwhelming desire for more, which took me away from the experience I was having, took me out of the present moment that was so joyful, and put me in the future that was neither as real nor as satisfying, a future dependent on blueberries that I didn't have. The physical sensations in my body went from warm, spacious, easeful, and joyful to contracted, focused, and not at all present.

When I noticed these physical contractions, I took a deep breath and looked at my husband's smile as he ate a few more berries. And then I refocused my attention onto the present moment, finding total contentment and joy again as I ate another sweet, luscious, blueberry.

REBEL

I ONCE HEARD A STORY ABOUT NATIVE PEOPLES not recognizing that colonists were sailing toward their shores. They didn't see them in the distance because, although they were familiar with dugouts and other canoe-type boats, they had never seen sails or sailboats. They literally did not see the sailboats on the horizon because they had never had the experience of seeing one before, and therefore, this image or thing was not in their consciousness, and they could not comprehend it. So, they disregarded it.

I could never confirm the truth of this story, but I found this metaphor of not seeing what we don't know (or don't want to know) to be true in my own experience.

During my Mindfulness-based Behavior Change training program, I was asked to take a quiz called the Four Tendencies developed by Gretchen Rubin. It asks twelve questions to determine how you respond to expectations and suggests that the answer influences your everyday behavior. The four possibilities are upholders, questioners, obligers, and rebels.

When I took the test, I was mostly a questioner. That wasn't a surprise to me. As a child, I was often told things that didn't make sense to me or that I didn't agree with, so I was always seeking and exploring other possible explanations. As I grew up, I often got myself in trouble at work or with acquaintances because I always asked for more information or clarity around their statements, beliefs, and perspectives.

Later that year, I was teaching the Mindfulness-based Behavior Change Program, and during class, we discussed one student's results of Rubin's test. This individual mentioned that she had one predominant tendency but also had a second strong tendency.

When she said that, it joggled my mind because it reminded me that I was sixty-five percent questioner, but as I reflected, I couldn't remember what my other tendency was. I visualized the results in my mind and could see the page on the screen, but literally couldn't "see" what the second tendency was. So, when I got home, I took the test again, and I came out sixty-five percent questioner and thirty-five percent rebel.

Rebel? I couldn't possibly be a rebel!

Not until that moment was I able to see that I have always been a rebel because, until that moment, it was not an acceptable possibility in my worldview. I was the firstborn of older, immigrant parents, and the only options in life were to hold the line, get an education (college) in a career that was stable (nursing), and make a living as soon as you graduated. I grew up in the 1960s, and I was so straight compared to my peers that there was no doubt to me that I was anything but a rebel. I maintained that worldview throughout my life, continuing to do what was expected of me, checking all the "right boxes," or at least, so I thought, even though I often felt like a square peg in a round hole.

With this insight, I could finally "see" that I am indeed a rebel. Not in the sense of doing anything illegal or dyeing my hair pink. But I have often quietly resisted or defied authority, social norms, and conventions. I tend to be independent, non-conformist, and anti-authoritarian, and have always sought to create my own path in life. I finally saw all the moments that I disagreed with others and got myself into trouble with my parents and my bosses as a reflection of being a rebel. Like when I questioned the expertise and commitment of a new administrator. No one else seemed concerned about her despite her reputation for being authoritarian. Or when I fought with the head of the department about him wanting me to ignore a state mandate. He suggested that "I work around it" or lose my job. Or arguing against nominating a board member who "knew the chairman" and had a conflict of interest. I've had numerous careers, moving on when I was most accomplished or something else interested me, without concern for how it would impact my income or my life.

As I reflect on Rubin's categories, I'd like to offer another perspective on my findings. Although I navigated my life as a questioner, I'm realizing now that the questioner category may actually be a socially acceptable rebel.

Did I just rearrange Rubin's categories? Of course, I did. That's because I'm a rebel.

IN A HURRY

As I looked into the distance, I could see a line of cars that seemed to go on forever. I was in the extreme right lane, stuck in traffic on the highway. We were only inching along. Scanning the traffic, I saw a car up ahead parked in the breakdown lane with the lights flashing. Even from a distance, the car looked tired with its fender askew and a different color trunk. A woman stood next to it. She looked a bit like her VW, small, bent over, and older. I was concerned about her as it was cold out and she only had a lightweight jacket on. My mind began to spin; what happened to her car, did she have a phone, had she called AAA or a friend or relative, why hadn't someone pulled over!

I was in a hurry. I needed to get into town to teach a Mindfulness-based Stress Reduction (MBSR) course. MBSR is an eight-week program designed to identify and work with one's perceived stressors. I recognized I was stressed because I was gripping the wheel and clenching my jaw. I did not want to be late. So, I drew on some of the skills I would be teaching. I took a couple of long, deep breaths and, as I exhaled, released some of the tension in my body.

As I got closer to her, the traffic eased up, and I was able to pick up speed.

I finally got to where the disabled car was parked, and I drove… right… by…... her.

But I was in a hurry!

OMG! I drove right by her!

According to scientific research, this isn't surprising. In the 1970s, two Princeton social psychologists tested the effects of the perception of time pressure on our likelihood of helping others. They looked at the probability of forty theology students helping another individual in need. The students were to go from one building to another and encounter an actor "sitting slumped in a doorway, head down, eyes closed, not moving." The actor coughed as the students walked by him to draw the students' attention. Students in a hurry to reach their destination were more likely to pass by without stopping. Some students were even going to give a short talk on the parable of the Good Samaritan; this made no difference in the likelihood of their giving the person help.

As I drove by, I felt the dissonance in my body and mind right away. My mind told me, "She's fine, someone else will stop, she's just waiting for AAA. She's fine. I don't have time to stop. I can't be late."

As my mind told me to keep going, my body said

the opposite. My whole body tensed, my breathing grew shallow again, and I gripped the wheel so hard my hands hurt. My body was screaming, "You didn't just do that, did you?"

I realized that I wouldn't be able to face myself later if I continued into town. So, I got off at the next exit, turned around, pulled back into the traffic, made my way back to the woman, and pulled over. I noticed she had put on another layer of clothing. I got out of the car and asked her if she needed anything. As I spoke with her, another person pulled over. She thanked us both, and as we stood there, a tow truck arrived. I was so relieved. I could now leave because I still had this nagging feeling that being late for my class was not acceptable. I had a responsibility to be there on time. I noticed the judgment I had about wasting time by going back to the woman with the broken-down car, especially since a tow truck arrived while I was there. I got into my car and headed to class. I was a bit late, but when I arrived, I experienced a feeling of relief and was glad for the decision I made. The dissonance had gone away. I felt more aligned with my values and ethics, even though my conditioned mind was still trying to make me feel guilty about being late for class and wasting time by going back.

When I got to class, everyone was concerned that I arrived late, so I told them of my experience. We had the opportunity to explore the situation, our feelings around it, perceived external expectations, internal expectations, and how we might or might not respond based on our values. And how sometimes these values can collide, as they did for me, not only when I drove past the woman but also as I went back to see if I could help. And how awareness can help us see the difference, help us recognize our sometimes-conflicted nature, and lead us to make more fully informed and more humane decisions, even if we are in a hurry.

SENSATIONS

MY STOMACH FELT LIKE IT WAS CLENCHED IN A vise grip, twisting around and around on itself. Nauseated, dizzy, my head pounding, body weighed down with extreme fatigue, and struggling through thick clouds of brain fog, I could barely stand up and walk from the living room to the kitchen, a journey that left me so exhausted I then needed to sit down again. Without the energy to collect and articulate my thoughts, conversing with my husband was almost impossible. This crippling condition would sweep over me sporadically, seemingly out of nowhere, last a few days, and then ebb slowly away.

I spent a lot of time at first avoiding and distracting myself from the pain and discomfort I was experiencing. It was easy in the beginning because these symptoms were intermittent and workable. But then they became stronger, more frequent, and adversely affected my everyday life. Over the last few years, I had felt unpredictably lousy and didn't have the energy to do all the things I needed to accomplish. So, I did what my meditation practice invites me to do: not only notice and turn towards what is pleasant in my life, but also turn towards that which is unpleasant and get to know it *really well*, with curiosity and without judgment. To know it as it actually is, rather than how I think about it, as in *"Oh, no! Here it comes again, I can't deal with this. This time it won't go away."* The practice invites me to move away from the dialogue in my head and drop down into my body and actually feel the sensations.

So, I did. I got to know the actual sensations of my experience: twisting, squeezing, bloating, crushing, nausea, dizziness, and heaviness. I noticed how each symptom changed and shifted. I learned that the abdominal cramps came and went. That the headache was a dull throbbing. And I noticed when it wasn't there. And noticing too, that when I brought compassion and attention to these unpleasant sensations, the frantic and fearful mind states that accompanied them faded.

And although I got to know the sensations well, I could not determine what might be causing them. So, I sought help.

I went to the doctor. *"You have migraines. Here, take this medication."* What? My headaches are the least of my symptoms.

I told my therapist. *"You're having a psychobiological response to childhood trauma."* Really? I've done all this work, and only now I'm getting physical symptoms?

Maybe I had post-exertional malaise. It seemed that

the weekends when my husband and I hiked, I would drive home on Monday in a stupor and couldn't find the energy to unpack my bags until the next morning. But yet, there were occasions when I completed a high-intensity interval training session and felt fine.

What other information could I glean when I turned towards the unpleasant to help me solve this?

Turns out I had enough information. The answer came as I chatted with a niece whom I hadn't seen for a while. She described having an illness that took three months to diagnose. As she listed her symptoms, I realized she was describing the same symptoms I was having. And she was diagnosed with celiac disease.

OMG! I never considered that my symptoms could be due to a food allergy. But now it made sense. Every weekend that we hiked, I'd make pasta for dinner on Saturday. Every Sunday, I thought I was tired from the previous day's hike and fatigued from the weekend as I drove home on Monday.

So, I did an experiment. I didn't eat gluten for two weeks. No nausea, dizziness, or headaches! Four weeks. No twisting, squeezing, or bloating. Six weeks. No fatigue, aches, or brain fog. And I continue to be symptom-free! I am gluten intolerant!

A few months later, I did another experiment. I wondered what would occur if I went to my favorite French bakery. What would happen to the joy and connection that I experienced in the past? I went because I wanted to pick up a loaf of sourdough bread that my husband really likes. I must admit, I was a bit apprehensive since I can't eat gluten anymore. As I entered the bakery, I brought my awareness to the sensations that were present. I noticed a contraction in my stomach, and I was holding my breath. But there were other sensations that I noticed after I moved away from the fear I was creating in my mind and just stayed with the awareness of the physical sensations. As I stood in line to be waited on, I engaged with all my senses. First, I noticed all the wonderful smells that can only be found in a bakery. I took a deep breath. Is it the sourdough starter that gives off that sweet scent? And so many different-shaped and colored foods! There were croissants, regular and chocolate, apple, pear, and blueberry tarts, country sourdough bread, olive bread, baguettes, and more, all made in-house that morning. I allowed my eyes to take in the colors, shapes, and textures.

The owner greeted me, "Bonjour! Que voulez-vous, Madame?"

"Just the country loaf, please."

"Voila!" he said as he handed me the bag that contained the fresh bread. It was still warm.

"Merci!" I replied.

As I left the bakery, I reflected on the sensations that were present, such as expansiveness and warmth. I realized that there was so much more happening in my experience than just choosing something to eat. The sensation that was most evident and vivid was that of satiety, even though I hadn't eaten a thing. A feast for the senses without ever taking a bite.

A BLANK PAGE

I'M SITTING HERE LOOKING AT A BLANK PAGE ON my computer screen. My writing assignment is due later today, and my mind is as blank as my screen.

I'm starting from a creative deficit. After freshman year in college, when I took my last English class, any writing skills I had atrophied because I no longer used them. I was oriented differently to the written word because I was a surgical ICU nurse and then a nurse anesthetist. We used SMS and emojis in the hospital long before the internet to get our point across quickly and efficiently. After my nursing career, I wrote research articles as an epidemiologist and reviewed them as an editor for Medscape. But these were written in template form, and even then, I was known to be terse.

I keep at it because writing is awakening parts of me that have been silent for too long. I feel seen and heard when I write. Each sentence has a feeling of expansiveness and possibility. I can be fully immersed in my own experience in my own time without commentary or opinions from others. I can reflect and see how a story lands… joy, vulnerability, surprise, curiosity.

From a scientific perspective, writing exercises our cognitive abilities and forms new neural pathways, and although I can't feel that happening, I feel something different when I write, a settling, a feeling of accomplishment, and of being heard.

Even with this knowledge, I sit here and still can't come up with anything, and I'm starting to get frustrated and a little bit anxious. My body feels heavy, my breathing is shallow, and my fingers feel like concrete. I can feel my jaw tense. I know if I stay in this mind state, I won't produce anything. I'll shut down completely, erasing any possibility of being creative or writing anything. So, I pause and lean into my mindfulness practice.

First, I am mindful that I am shutting down. This awareness is key because it stops me from getting caught up in the negativity and allows me to investigate what is contributing to my shutting down.

With investigation, I quickly identify that I am denigrating myself for not taking the advice of many authors and teachers, which is to designate a time and place and write consistently over many weeks and months. If I had, I reasoned, I would be prepared for this writing assignment. But I never embraced the idea of a consistent writing practice because I don't tend to follow rules. I'm a bit of a rebel and will go about a task differently than everyone else, even if it makes it more difficult. I don't like being told what to do. A slight grin comes onto my face as I acknowledge this, and with that smile, I am no longer shut down. With that smile, there is a slight opening of my heart and mind, and I get motivated. "It's okay," my mind calmly said.

I can now take a deep breath and focus on the assignment. There is more spaciousness and equanimity available to me. Only then can I see what a blank page offers me, which is the opportunity to write about not being able to write, and so I begin…..

I'm sitting here looking at a blank page on my computer screen…. my relaxed fingers typing out the words as I continue to smile.

THE EXPERIENCE IS REAL,
BUT IS IT TRUE?

My husband was on his way home, and I was standing in the kitchen in a panic. I recognized this familiar feeling of fear, dread, and vigilance.

Panic is a visceral response; the tightening of the abdomen, chest, and throat, shallow breathing, feeling disconnected from the body, as well as a sense of helplessness and of wanting to disappear.

The sensations came on strong and clear. I recognized that part of me was no longer standing in the kitchen but transplanted to an earlier time. A time when the fear originated from the constant and relentless not knowing. Not knowing when my mother would explode in anger and become completely irrational. Not knowing what the consequences of her anger were going to be. Not knowing if what I did was "wrong" and even if it was "right," it wasn't good enough. Not knowing what to do or where to go to feel safe.

But in this moment, that was not what was happening. What was happening was that my husband's business was in crisis. He was okay, but his work environment was disruptive and unpleasant. More importantly, my husband is not irrational, angry, or a shouter. He is a kind, thoughtful person going through what, for him, was a very difficult time.

So, yes, it was difficult for him, but my feelings of hypervigilance and panic were not the appropriate response. What I was experiencing was a conditioned response of fear so well ingrained and insidious that I was still experiencing it even though my mother had been dead for more than forty years.

I could hear the garage door go up and the car pull in. Then the garage door came down. The house door opened. I was physically in a state of panic, but I could be present enough to see it happening. That it was my conditioning manifesting in my body due to my past. I understood that it was my husband coming in through the door, not my mother, and that this was not at all, in any way whatsoever, the same as what I had experienced as a child. I viewed this all from awareness. Awareness removed the veil from my eyes so that I could see it clearly.

Rather than getting stuck in the mire of my conditioning keeping me in an unskillful state, I realigned my actions to support me being in the present moment not just for myself but for my husband, by feeling my feet on the ground, taking slow deep breaths, giving my husband a kiss, feeling the physical sensations of contact between our two bodies, and being grateful for being able to connect with this moment in this way. I shifted my awareness so that now my experience was not only true, but real; not there, but here; not then, but now.

IN THE MIDST

"HOLD ON! EXCUSE ME FOR A MOMENT!" BETTY exclaimed to me. I was teaching an online mindfulness course, and Betty was one of twenty participants. This was our second session, and I was doing an inquiry about her experience with mindfulness when she interrupted me. She then proceeded to tell Sarah, who was another participant in the class, that what she had just written in the chat was inappropriate and disrespectful to the group.

Betty had taken me off guard, and I had no idea what was going on, so I looked at the chat, and it said something to the effect of "Chewing gum on screen is rude. Either go off-screen or ditch the gum!" It was addressed to everyone.

I had indeed noticed the gum chewer during the opening meditation. Cynthia was making huge bubbles on screen, which were distracting. But I also noticed that during the meditation, she was restless and that she was shedding some tears. I decided to let it go and connect with her after class.

But now we were in the midst of a confrontation. Betty and Sarah exchanged some additional words where neither one backed down from their positions, and Cynthia quietly defended herself by saying, "I was chewing gum to try to control my anxiety."

I took a deep breath and let the situation make itself clear to me. The usual way of responding would be to assign blame and tell each individual which aspects of what they did were wrong or how they hadn't followed the guidelines that were previously established. And that was legitimate. I was the teacher and needed to address what had become disruptive to everyone. Or should I simply take the blame for not addressing the gum chewing at the beginning of class?

I decided to do neither. Instead, I invited everyone in the class to pause.

Then I asked them to bring their attention to the thoughts and emotions that were arising. *Did you have an opinion of who was right and who was wrong?*

What other thoughts arose?

What physical sensations were in your body as you brought awareness to your thoughts?

Were there any places of constriction? Perhaps in the belly or in the throat?

Were you holding your breath? Was your breath shallow?
Did you want to hide or defend anyone?

Were you restless? How did that feel in the body?

The truth was nobody meant to be rude or confrontational. I confirmed this with all three individuals after class. Then how did this situation come about, even though no one meant any harm? Each person was simply responding to their own ideas and opinions of right and wrong in their usual habitual manner, but was unaware of the consequences of their actions. If we look at it from each participant's perspective, Cynthia was so distressed she didn't notice how she looked on screen. Sarah felt Cynthia was not conforming to standard Zoom etiquette, and Betty stepped in to right a perceived wrong.

This situation was a perfect opportunity to explore what we were learning in this mindfulness course! Class 1 was an exploration of being on automatic pilot and how we can get carried away by our habitual reactions. Class 2 was using the body and its sensations as an anchor and early warning message system identifying stress, anxiety, and fatigue, and here we were in the midst of a real-world, real-time example.

Doing this, I invited everyone to look at the situation through the lens of mindfulness. According to the American Psychological Association, mindfulness is *"awareness of one's internal states and surroundings. Mindfulness can help people avoid destructive or automatic habits and responses by learning to observe their thoughts, emotions, and other present-moment experiences without judging or reacting to them."*

So, with this approach, there was no blame or judgment. It was simply an opportunity to reflect on what had occurred to understand our reactivity, whether or not we contributed to the situation. What were the habitual patterns that arose? Could we bring in some compassion for ourselves and others since we are all trying to do our best?

So how did this teaching moment land? As it turned out, Cynthia never returned to class despite my encouragement, and I don't know if she ever found any relief from her anxiety. Sarah made it clear she was not apologizing for her comments, but I also found out her husband was quite ill, and although his immunotherapy was successful, he had a long road ahead. Betty felt remorse and denigrated herself for jumping in and berating Sarah. Another participant noted in the class evaluation that a *"chat dialogue arose during one class that I didn't feel was handled appropriately."* And I paused and took a couple of deep breaths, trying to find some peace in the midst of it all.

NOT GOOD ENOUGH

Recently, an email popped up on my screen from my supervisor with the subject line Course Evaluations. I opened the email and it read: *"Please do give the attached program evaluation summary report a thorough read and let me know if you have any questions. As you'll see, there was some constructive feedback…"*

As soon as I read these two sentences, I paused, sat back, and waited for it. And I didn't need to wait long….

Crap!

I got a bad review!

They don't think I'm good enough.

I failed.

It's my fault.

They're going to fire me.

I'm ashamed.

Right on cue. This familiar dialogue of *never good enough*. For the longest time, I believed this story. Why not? I wasn't given a lot of kudos as a child, and our society and institutions tend to be hard on us, especially women, to be perfect, produce at work, and do it all. This perspective was always present and influencing every aspect of my life. Trying too hard and not caring for myself, being despondent when I "failed" or not noticing and celebrating what I accomplished.

When the *never good enough* would make itself known, I'd get agitated and restless, as well as feel constriction in my body, and I'd want to hide. This was accompanied by hypervigilance. Physically, there would be an increase in my respiratory rate but a decrease in volume, tension in my jaw, and I would lose my appetite.

But this time my response was very different due to my awareness of this tendency. The commentary in my mind was loud and strong, but the visceral response was almost negligible...almost. There was a very mild heaviness that I noticed and that followed me around for a while, but rather than push it away, I acknowledged it. "Oh, yeah, that old stuff."

I also read the actual evaluations, and the core of the comments was not directed at me. And what was directed at me had been addressed during class. I found it more interesting than distressing that this issue, which I thought was resolved, was brought up again.

But a few hours later, I noticed I was telling myself an old story of fixing what I thought was wrong (the individuals who wrote the evaluations) to soothe myself. This organism's (mine) desire to care for itself was so strong that it was still trying to support me with its old, conditioned responses.

That's how we humans are. We learn something and then rely on it again and again, even though it may no longer be appropriate or helpful.

And so, with awareness, I leaned into my practice so that I didn't go down the rabbit hole of shame and blame. I leaned in by being aware of these thoughts and then considered the choices I had to disengage from the emotional responses that were arising and that were so toxic. To do that, I dropped down into the body and felt the breath coming into and out of the body, and felt my feet on the ground and my hands touching each other. I disengaged from the thoughts by noticing what was in my visual field... perhaps even naming what I saw. I consciously turned my thoughts to things that are more wholesome, such as gratitude for the opportunity to teach, appreciation for the support of my colleagues, or curiosity about the participants' comments.

A few months later, I read another group of course evaluations, and one in particular stood out: "*Priscilla did an outstanding job of leading the class. She showed wisdom, expertise, compassion, kindness, and humor in her leadership style.*" I paused, sat back, and waited for it. And I didn't need to wait long for the voice that said, "*You are good enough and more!*"

SAVOR THE JOY

Joy comes in different flavors: delight, tranquility, awe, passion, thrill, triumph, bliss, peace, calm, laughter, exuberance, appreciation, gratitude, elation, and rejoicing. Joy balances the mind when it is too dull or disengaged, and it is a benefit of meditation practice as well as a factor for well-being. And to attain deep states of meditative concentration called jhanas, joy plays a prominent role.

For most of us, joy simply feels good. But as humans, we tend to either not pay attention to moments of joy or we try to grasp those moments after they've occurred. We don't stay with these moments as they are happening. This is due to our innate negativity bias that wants to protect us against harm by focusing on situations that are unpleasant or may put us at risk. To counter this biological survival mechanism, we need to be conscious of and present for the feelings that joy evokes and savor them.

I practiced staying with the feelings of joy while making a basket with a small group of adults at our local arts center. We worked with willow, an incredibly tactile material. It comes in long stalks, and when you engage with it, it has a slight heft but also an easy flexibility after it is soaked in water. Bending the stalk back and forth as I prepared to work with it, a subtle contentment grew. Willow is known to have a minty or wintergreen scent. To me, it smells like soap, and with each breath, I savored its fragrance. It comes in an array of colors: yellow, red, black, brown, green, and purple-red, and taking in this multi-hued palette created a soft visual delight. It's a natural, sustainable fiber that has incredible, natural beauty, which fosters a gentle sense of connection to the earth. As our baskets started to take shape, everyone in the class had smiles on their faces reflecting the delight of being part of the process of this exquisite material taking shape into something not only practical but also creative.

I pay attention to the joy that arises during my daily meditation practice. I usually sit on the floor cross-legged and have been doing so for twenty years. I have a favorite cushion that I sit on, and this familiar posture results in a somatic response of ease and relaxation, almost like my body saying ahhhh. My space is private with just what I need and nothing more, creating a safe and comfortable environment. It is also full of natural light with the sun bouncing on different surfaces and warming my body early in the morning. As I take in the room, I feel an expansiveness in my body and a natural wakefulness and tranquility. I experience a sweet bliss even though my mind might be busy with lots of thoughts. In the past, I would be distressed by my racing mind, but I now simply greet those racing thoughts like the old friends they are. My mind chatters in the background, and I smile as I focus on my breath. I have so much appreciation for the practice.

More moments of joy....

It was late November in New Hampshire. About twenty-five degrees Fahrenheit, sunny with no wind. A perfect day to hike. As we made our way up the mountain, I could feel the coolness of the air on my face, but my body was warm and cozy in the many layers of fleece. My attention turned toward the natural beauty in the woods. I took in the sounds of the river, the dappled sunlight in the forest, and the snow crunching under my feet as I relaxed into the rhythm of lifting and placing my feet on the trail.

Occasionally, we would pass other hikers coming down the trail, and we greeted one another. Today, we all commented on the beauty of the day and how we were all so grateful to be outdoors to enjoy it. As I looked ahead, I could see a couple making their way down the mountain, and they had a dog with them. The dog couldn't have been happier, running down the trail and then back up again towards its owners. Seeing her joy made me smile. As the dog came down the hill toward me, she looked at me and hesitated, but I encouraged her over. I felt open-hearted and delighted to be with her exuberance.

She was looking for some free pets, and I was happy to accommodate. Her tail wagged, and she snuggled into my leg. I could feel this joy as warmth and contentment, and if I had a tail, I'd be wagging it too.

I don't usually have the radio on in the car, but I did on this three-hour drive up north. Aretha Franklin singing "Bridge Over Troubled Waters" came on, and as she hit a high note, my entire body responded. It was as if the song entered my body, and my body said yes. Hearing the musicality of her voice as she expressed the lyrics with emotional depth and intensity, I noticed a gasp, felt chills, a stirring of the heart, and full appreciation for this extraordinary, unexpected moment. Awe, thrills, and rapture. No mind involved at all, just a complete bodily experience savoring this indescribably joyful moment.

IT'S ALL MEDITATION

When I first started meditating, I went on a few week-long retreats, and on returning home, I'd always ask the question, *"How do I bring what I learned on retreat home?"* Now, as I reflect on those experiences, that really wasn't the question I was asking. I was really asking, *"How can I get rid of the discomfort of everyday life, after I found peace and calm on retreat?"*

Although meditation practice on retreat can be peaceful and a modicum of calm is an important element to be able to cultivate concentration, there is no guarantee that it will happen. Rather, mindfulness meditation asks us to be with what is present in this moment, whether it is calm, confusion, a restless mind, body aches, bliss, or anything else that arises. In this way, we practice being with what is here right now by not pushing away the unpleasant or grasping for the pleasant. So, whether you are on retreat or feeding the dog, the intention is to be with your heart and mind as it is and investigate it. And as you do, you become more comfortable with what's uncomfortable by observing what arises rather than getting caught up in it.

And as one practices, whether with sitting meditation or paying attention to activities of daily living, mindfulness and its associated characteristics (generosity, virtue, renunciation, wisdom, energy, patience, truthfulness, determination, lovingkindness, and equanimity) become stronger and more consistent. And then with time, your practice during retreat isn't any different from your practice during your daily life. They become seamless. It's all meditation.

I saw how my practice has gotten more seamless over a weekend in upstate New York.

Traffic is my Achilles heel. My attitude is that traffic is a waste of time, and the sooner I can get to where I am going, the better. To accomplish this in the most efficient manner means that everyone needs to get out of my way. On this particular drive, I expected to be on the road for five hours, but it turned out to be seven. Unfortunately, I was stuck in Friday afternoon traffic. The stop-and-go was torturous, and I could barely breathe; my body was so tense. When I finally acknowledged it, I said, *"Yes, you don't like it, but can you be with it?"* My answer was *"Yes"* as I tapped into a wellspring of patience and innate wisdom.

I think that acknowledgement supported me when we were stopped dead before getting off the exit for Route 87. The traffic had stopped after we crested a hill, so drivers couldn't anticipate the delay. I was in the second lane from the left of five lanes and heard that familiar screech of brakes. When I looked to the left, to the outer lane, I saw a car trying to stop but couldn't. You could smell the brakes smoldering as they were asked to go beyond their normal capacity, and what was visible was the smoke rising from the car and the road. We were all lucky he had a shoulder to veer off into. The whole episode happened in slow motion; a few seconds lengthened into eternity, and the image is still vivid in my mind. The car he almost hit then scooted behind me as my lane of traffic slowly moved forward. I took it in and only felt relief and calm. Equanimity arising on its own. Perhaps I wouldn't have been as equanimous if the cars had crashed, or if I were in the outer lane.

I also noticed the seamless integration during a bike ride through agricultural land in upstate New York. It was a perfect day to cycle, and the route was serene and beautiful. There were literally a hundred barns on the green rolling hills as we made our way along the route, stopping at orchards, dairy farms, a learning museum, a brewery, a creamery, and animal farms. I was so present to my experience and had so much gratitude spending time outdoors in this bucolic setting. At the end of the ride, we all spent time at the brewery, listening to music, sharing stories, and I enjoyed one of the best gluten-free meals I've ever had. Tons of veggies with a wonderful sauce topped off the day. Being present for and luxuri-ating in this idyllic environment.

The anger, the joy, the confusion, the sit, the argument, the hug; it's all meditation if we are aware of our experience both externally and what arises internally. Awareness grounds us as these mind states arise; we know we are happy, angry, sad, or confused. Wisdom arises as well, and if we pay attention to wisdom, it can help us recognize our relationship to our experience and discriminate between reacting and responding. And from there, our wholesome actions can naturally arise in the moment, just as it is, because it's all meditation.

ABOUT THE AUTHOR

PRISCILLA SZNEKE has practiced in the Insight meditation tradition for over twenty years, which she is authorized to teach through the Spirit Rock Community Dharma Leaders Program. After a thirty-five-year career in healthcare as a nurse, epidemiologist, and medical editor, she transitioned to sharing mindfulness and meditation practices with others and has been doing so since 2009. This integration of life experiences and formal practice results in a unique perspective and depth of knowledge that informs her teaching.

Priscilla has facilitated a local sangha for more than

fifteen years and delivers an array of mindfulness-based programs. She holds certifications in Mindfulness-Based Stress Reduction (MBSR), Mindfulness-Based Blood Pressure Reduction (MB-BP), and Mindfulness-Based Eating Awareness Training (MB-EAT). She is a Qualified Behavior Change Facilitator and is authorized to teach Finding Peace in a Frantic World. Priscilla has provided these and other mindfulness-based interventions (MBIs) aimed at promoting well-being and resilience to groups in academic institutions and non-profit organizations, to corporate clients, community groups, and individuals. Currently, she teaches these evidence-based MBIs through the School of Professional Studies at Brown University and serves as Adjunct Faculty at the Mindfulness Center at Brown University.

Her greatest happiness in offering these practices is witnessing how individuals integrate mindfulness and meditation into their lives and how that results in cultivating compassion, wisdom, and joy.

www.ingramcontent.com/pod-product-compliance
Lightning Source LLC
Chambersburg PA
CBHW051843090426
42736CB00011B/1928